THE IDEOLOGY
OF ADMINISTRATION

THE IDEOLOGY
OF ADMINISTRATION
AMERICAN AND SOVIET CASES

MICHAEL E. URBAN
State University of New York, Oswego

State University of New York Press

ALBANY

Published by
State University of New York Press, Albany

© 1982 State University of New York

For information, address State University of New York
Press, State University Plaza, Albany, N.Y., 12246

Library of Congress Cataloging in Publication Data
Urban, Michael E., 1947—
    The ideology of administration.

    1. Bureaucracy—United States. 2. Bureaucracy—
Soviet Union. 3. Industrial management—United
States. 4. Industrial management—Soviet Union.
I. Title.
HD38.4.U7   350'.000947   81-9035
ISBN 0-87395-556-0   AACR 2
ISBN 0-87395-557-9 (pbk.)

Contents

Acknowledgments

Having spent the better part of my research efforts over the past seven years on this study, I have, naturally, accumulated a substantial intellectual debt to a number of scholars. While none is culpable for the errors in judgment or fact which might remain in these pages, they are all responsible in innumerable ways, both direct and indirect, for what merit this work contains. I would like to express my gratitude specifically to the following individuals. First, I want to thank Roy Laird, Gary Wamsley, David Willer and Max Mote, who supervised various stages and aspects of my graduate work. I came to expect from all of these men nothing less than their sharpest criticism of my work together with an abiding intellectual support for my efforts. They gave me both cause to doubt and the confidence to pursue my ideas in the face of doubt.

Second, another group of scholars, men who were present at important junctures in the progress of my research, have earned my deep gratitude. These individuals, giving freely of their time, energy and knowledge, helped me through many conceptual bottlenecks, pointed out the pitfalls on this road or that, and contributed immeasurably to the joy of discovery which I experienced often enough in the course of my research. Here, I would like to thank in particular Stephen White, Hillel Ticktin, James White, Ron Perrin, Peter Koehn, William Scheuerman, Tsuyoshi Hasegawa and George Breslauer.

Third, my research in the Soviet Union benefitted enormously from the counsel of R. A. Safarov and A. A. Bezuglov. I owe a special debt of gratitude to G. V. Barabashev who taught me a great deal about the Soviet system and whose unflagging efforts were responsible for the success I had in negotiating the obstacles of the Soviet bureaucracy and in accomplishing more in the USSR than I had expected or otherwise could have hoped. I am sure that each of these scholars would disagree with much of my analysis of the Soviet system. Of greater import, however, is the consideration and respect which they showed in entertaining my questions and ideas, regardless of how sharply their perspectives might differ from mine.

Finally, my deepest gratitude goes to my family. My wife, Veronica, has developed over the period of my work the very countenance of understanding and patience. She certainly put up with more than could be expected of anyone, often living in far from comfortable circumstances such as those which befell us in Moscow, Leningrad and Glasgow, managing to make a family life where none seemed possible. My daughter, Emily, and son, George, put up with their share of it, too. Their sacrifices—whether, as Emily did, attending pre-school in a foreign country whose language she did not at first speak, or suppressing their natural vitality during winter's long house-bound months in order to give me the quiet which I needed to write—can be appreciated but never repaid.

The Ideology of Administration

Modern civilization depends largely on organizations as the most rational and efficient form of social organizations known . . . [serving] the needs of society and its citizens more efficiently than small and more natural human groupings such as families, friendship groups and communities.
—Amatai Etzioni

As given future goals become increasingly clear . . . social behavior may increasingly resemble that of a servomechanism in which guidance is reduced to control. . . . Action may then become a routine problem of technical administration. —C.R. Deckert

In the conditions of socialism arises the possibility of surmounting contradictions on the basis of the knowledge and conscious utilization of the laws of social development in the interests of the people. —M. A. Suslov

The distinguishing mark of the executive responsibility is that it requires not merely conformance to a complex code of morals but also the creation of a moral code for others . . . that will result in subordinating individual interests and the minor dictates of personal codes to the good of the cooperative whole. —Chester Barnard

[The administrative leader] is a principled person, able to subordinate his own interests to the collective . . . a modest and simple person in dealings with other people, regardless of their station in the organization, showing unceasing concern for people and their welfare. —I. Ya. Kasitskii

Public executives . . . are responsible for the operation of our society; they cannot wait around for somebody to tell them what to do. If they don't know the answers, we're lost. —E. P. Dvorin and R. H. Simmons

Many objective factors . . . require the creation of a stable and qualified personnel of the state organs. . . . Hence, a specialization of the functions of administration must be deduced, requiring special knowledge and practice. . . Therefore, the entire people who hold power entrust to a specific category of workers the fulfillment of the function of administration.
—Yu. A. Tikhomirov

Introduction

This study began with the disturbing perplexity which I experienced on first encountering statements such as those above. Perplexity led to more reading in the literature on administration, producing, in turn, even more perplexity. Why all the double talk? How can the realization of human freedom be rendered synonymous with increasing the scope and power of bureaucratic control? How is it that government by administration is extolled as the fulfillment of democracy's promise? More, in reading both American and Soviet professional literature on administration I repeatedly noticed the same themes, the same desiderata and, indeed, much of the same double talk. In order to comprehend the significance of such statements appearing in societies as dissimilar (on the surface, at least) as the US and the USSR, I set about constructing some working hypotheses. The first of these was the decision to treat what is loosely called "administrative theory" as administrative ideology. This does not imply a mere pejorative renaming. As Max Horkheimer has pointed out:

> To say it is ideological is not to say that its practitioners are not concerned with pure truth. Every human way of acting which hides the true nature of society, built as it is on contrarities, is ideological, and the claim that philosophical, moral and religious acts of faith, scientific theories, legal maxims and cultural institutions have this function is not an attack on the character of those who originate them but only states the objective role such realities play in society.[1]

To be sure, the perspective represented by statements such as those cited at the end of this introduction would likely deny to "ideology," at least in the full and critical sense of that term, any place in the modern world. Yet the "end of ideology" persuasion is nothing other than the triumph of ideological thought. It conceals behind its bragging banner a series of choices: to quit reflection for application and action, to eschew interpretation and embrace the precision and certainty of "science," to degrade, in fact, "mere" ideas in favor of "real" accomplishments (expressed no more clearly than by the voice of the jet airliner overhead which sings its mighty deed to me as I write these lines). The decision to treat the corpus of the professional literature on administration as the written expression of administrative ideology implies a critical, interpretive posture toward it.

Second, the *significance* (or "meaning") of administrative ideology would lie between the *description* of its contents and the *explanation* of its existence and of the forms which it takes. One never steps into the same river twice, and one never comes to the reading of a text in quite the same way, or as quite the same reader, as was true the day before. "Reading," Colin Summer reminds us, "is a practice within which we become aware of significance or meaning in social phenomena."[2] This is an ongoing process wherein significance emerges over a period of time, over a series of recognitions and misrecognitions, interpretations and reinterpretations. Establishing "significance" means, in short, that we understand what the speaker or writer means by adopting as best we can his viewpoint.[3]

Third, the analysis of ideology cannot stop at the level of significance or meaning; rather ideology must be located in the world and seen as a particular expression of social life. Explanation, here, establishes the connections between the structure of power and privilege in a social order and the manner in which that social order is comprehended and legitimated through the prism of ideology.

Finally, I chose the United States and the Soviet Union as cases for a comparative study of the ideology of administration. This selection was predicated on an interest in discovering something about the tendency toward bureaucracy in the modern world, a tendency first grasped by Max Weber.[4] These cases represent variants of this tendency. My purpose is not to argue for or against some sort of convergence. Rather, it is to examine two types of bureaucratic societies from the standpoint of the ideologies generated by each and, making allowances for contextual differences, to focus on what they appear to hold in common. In order to do so, some common frame of reference is, of course, necessary. Categories such as capitalist/socialist, Western/Eastern, not to mention totalitarian/democratic, would simply not acount for what I had encountered in the professional literature in each country. I was, therefore, attracted to the concept of "modern industrial society" and to a problematic associated with it; *viz.*, ideology and bureaucracy, a mode of knowing and an attendant form of social life, which comprise a dialectical unity within the modern industrial order.

The thesis developed in this work refers to an *aspect* of this unity, namely, "administrative ideology." Such pertains to the ideational systems of salient bureaucratic actors, *viz.*, "administrators." In a preliminary manner, the thesis can be simply put as follows: Contradictions inherent within the practice of administration find expression and resolution at the level of symbols (ideology) which, as mediators between the world of action and the realm of reflection, serve to stabilize the administrative role.

The meaning of this thesis depends on an "unravelling" of the relations between the aspect (the ideology of administration) and the problematic (ideology and bureaucracy in modern industrial society). This unravelling comprises the first part of the book. The intention therein is to seek out the form of the relations or inter-connections between administrative ideology and the structures of power built within and around the administrative role. The idea of unravelling can likewise express a process of explanation wherein the phenomenon under investigation is situated within a larger theoretical framework. Explanation occurs, in this respect, as logically related theoretical categories subsume the empirical ones presented in outline in Part One. The empirical material is discussed in more detail in the second part, but at this stage it appears in a form ordered by the foregoing theoretical development. As such, Part Two is concerned to reconstruct from administrative literature—the "raw material"—a pattern of ideological responses to the contradictions developed in Part One. This pattern is also grounded empirically by means of interviews which I have conducted with administrators in the US and the USSR.

Part One
The General Ideology of Administration

1
Administrative Ideology: Concept and Method

What is ideology? Ideology is an oft used term. Its currency, how-ever, need not suggest that the concept "ideology" is understood in a uniform manner. Far from it. One reason for dissensus is, of course, the critical and *reflexive* nature of the concept itself. "The educator himself needs educating,"[1] as Marx wrote. Another might be the etherial nature of the subject matter, ideas in connection, which indeed only becomes a matter for study upon the decision of the investigator to interpret an idea as a datum and to treat such data as an ideology. In the process, investigation involves coaxing, as it were, more meaning out of the ideas than they would otherwise be prepared to admit.

The word "ideology" has been employed by some recent writers as an antonym for pragmatic thinking.[2] Clearheaded, empirical, dispassionate, practical and open-ended would, in this view, count as qualities foreign to the ideological frame of mind. Therefore, on meeting ideas in connection, particularly ideas which in some way express social values, we have the assurance of knowing that it is "ideology" with which we are dealing.

This more or less conventional notion of ideology has been appro-priated to the study of bureaucracy, yielding the term, "bureaucratic ideology." No doubt, the idea that administrative bodies tend to have relatively coherent belief systems, identifiable rituals and inte-grating symbols which bear upon the operation of these bodies, represents an advance over yesterday's wisdom which, by accord-ing administrative agencies a "neutral" status, implied that they

3

were simply the objects of political power and almost infinitely malleable objects at that. The recent refinements in thinking about both bureaucracy and ideology seem to tell us something about the behavior of large organizations. However, the same cannot be said with respect to "ideology," for, if anything, this concept, when conjoined with the adjective "bureaucratic," has been emptied of much of its meaning and, consequently, its critical power.

Anthony Downs, for instance, defines "bureaucratic ideology" as:

a verbal image of that portion of the good society relevant to the functions of the particular bureau concerned, plus the chief means of constructing that portion.[3]

This usage of the term "ideology" is certainly in consonance with the conventional strictures on "concept formation" common to the contemporary positivism of social science methodology.[4] It provides a clear empirical referent ("verbal image") and could conceivably be of use in the task of organizing data relevant to the concept itself. The problem, however, is that in defining "bureaucratic ideology" in this way, the political-philosophical relevance of the term, the problematic which has historically accompanied its usage, is simply ignored. That which the analysis of ideology has been most intent on investigating—the relationship between social power in a given society and how that social power is understood and misunderstood within that society—is, under this concept of ideology, screened out. Take, for example, Downs' "verbal image" which is "relevant to the functions of the particular bureau concerned." Despite the merits which this approach might have with respect to understanding "the particular bureau," it is unable to address what surely are the more important questions: Has a general ideology emerged as an analogue to the general bureaucratization of society in this century? If such is true, how does this ideology interpret and stabilize such bureaucratization? These queries direct our attention beyond the given, beyond "the particular bureau." They would prompt us, instead, to begin thinking about a process which has radically transformed social relations and our attendant form of life in what may presently be called "modern industrial societies." More, they would bring into focus the manner in which this process has been portrayed in thought by those most directly involved in it. The examination of ideology of administration leads, albeit indirectly, back to the way in which life is ordered, understood and carried on in modern industrial society. In deciphering it, in tracing the forms of this ideology back to their bases in social practice, we are also seeking its explanation. The conventional concept of "bureaucratic ideology" is not adequate to such a task. At best, it leads to an insufficient comprehension of the subject. At worst, it amounts to a trivialization of the concept such as to render it useless to any scholarly enterprise seeking to do more than attach facile labels to whatever data happen to be handy.

A more satisfactory concept of ideology would require the restoration of two dimensions long associated with its usage outside the positivist camp: history and criticism.[5] These flow from the meaning of the concept "ideology" itself. That is, ideology refers to a more or less coherent set of ideas which are generated by real conditions of conflict or contradiction obtaining in society. Such ideas reflect this conflict, but in a refracted manner, so as to render it resolvable at the level of symbols. As such, ideologies simultaneously reveal and conceal something about the conditions which give them birth and, insofar as they conceal or obscure these conditions in thought, they tend to stabilize or perpetuate them in reality.[6] That such is not necessarily (or usually) undertaken consciously as a perpetration of deliberate falsehoods, or that ideologies may reflect a "partial reality" and be of service to instrumental action is largely beside the point.[7] What is important is the mediating role which ideologies play between the action of men, on the one hand, and that action as it is reflected in their minds on the other. As a mediator standing mid-way between thinking and doing, an ideology includes certain elements from its social context within the construction of symbolic forms; hence, an understanding of this context is indispensable to an understanding of the ideology itself. Inasmuch as ideology is rooted in the preservation of the *status quo*,[8] we can expect certain aspects of the social context to be hidden in and by the ideological form.[9] Consequently, a critical approach is essential for deciphering the set of clues, which an ideology provides, to the conditions of social conflict which, although obscured, ultimately stand behind the ideology. History and criticism are methodological guidelines along which an examination of ideology must procede. Before treating them in more detail, however, we might bring the concept of ideology into sharper focus.

Ideology, Myth and Symbols

Ideology, in the view of Juergen Habermas, counts as an instance of blocked or distorted communication.[10] Habermas has developed the thesis that all communications presuppose an orientation toward truth. This holds even for deliberately misleading statements (the extreme case) inasmuch as their feigned truthfulness is the means by which their communicator intends to deceive his audience. The truth orientation of an ideology is a partial one; it is blocked by the insistent presence of particular or "non-generalizable" interests which distort communication.[11] Building on this work, Alvin Gouldner[12] has argued that ideology is reason's bastard child. Ideology seeks to persuade rationally. It never claims the mantle of tradition or the authority of the speaker for its validity. Rather, it aims to convince its audience through the force of its own reasonable arguments. "Don't take my word for it," says Gouldner's ideologue, "consider the argument yourself and make up your own mind. I am confident that as a reasonable person you will accept it."

The particular interests embedded in an ideology, however, circumscribe its rational side and cripple its argumentative force. The point at which the generality of reason and the non-generalizable interests come into conflict is precisely the point at which an ideology's argumentative force is exhausted. If it is to persuade further in the face of this, ideology must contain another element, namely, symbology. It is through the peculiar nature of symbols and their operation in the mind that ideology surmounts its basis in particularistic material interests and reaches beyond these to become a social force. Hence, our analysis of ideology will join to the perspective of such thinkers as Habermas and Gouldner, who emphasize ideology's rational aspects, the insights of those who have concentrated on its symbolic content.

We might begin our discussion of the symbolic side of ideology by distinguishing between the related terms "sign" and "symbol." Whereas a sign is a concept (referring to an object or function) which is relatively unambiguous in its intention and meaning, a symbol is highly ambiguous and, as such, carries with it a multitude of meanings in a concentrated form.[13] Hence, as Philip Wheelwright has put it, symbols point beyond themselves; they mean more than they are, and they have the property "of *being more in intention than they are in existence.*"[14]

For our purposes here, two aspects of symbols as they are conjoined in an ideology deserve some attention. First, ideology, through its symbolic structures, serves to organize the perception and assessment of the world in a specific manner. In this respect, political ideology in the modern world resembles its counterpart, myth, in traditional society.[15] Ernst Cassirer has provided a number of penetrating and profound insights into the function of myth as an organizer of consciousness and of the world as apprehended by consciousness. The motive force in myth-making, he writes, is the "projection of man's social life." Hence, "not nature but society is the true model of myth."[16] Once projected in the form of symbols, however, myth seems to have a life of its own, to exist over and above the social life of men as an instructor, a guide, a judge. Yet even as myth severs its links with the concrete social world which gave it birth, it enters this world anew at the level of consciousness. "The mythical form of conception," Cassirer observes, "is not something super-added to certain definite *elements* of empirical existence; instead, the primary 'experience' itself is steeped in the imagery of myth and saturated with its atmosphere."[17] The symbols through which the world is perceived thereby account for the way in which the world "means" for the perceiver, the way in which it is understood and assessed. In the words of Claude Levi-Strauss, symbols "penetrate the screen of consciousness to carry the message directly to the unconscious [and] it is the effectiveness of symbols which guarantees the harmonious and parallel development of myth and action."[18]

In the same way that symbols may penetrate or elude the "screen of consciousness," the images which they carry are manifest to the mind not as what they are, images, but as realities.[19] As a result, the meaning of a symbol is merged with its context. The word "science," for instance, can act as such a symbol or mythical image. Its use as a symbol will empty it of the meaning[20] which it holds for those who actually practice science, and, so emptied, supply it with a penumbra of associations from its context (men in lab coats, exact knowledge, technological prowess, moon shots). Surrounded with such a contextual richness, the symbol acts as a form of "word magic" whereby the symbol and its referent are merged, and the mere presence of the symbol is comprehended as the presence of the thing itself.[21] This facet of symbols, as they appear in myth or ideology, clearly divides logical-discursive from mythical or ideological thinking,[22] and accounts for the peculiar potency of the latter as an agent which fixes both what is perceived and how it is evaluated in the social world.[23]

Second, ideology, as a social phenomenon, provides a certain symbolic adhesive which unites members in what M. M. Lewis has called "group mind."[24] For Lewis:

> Group mind is group behavior mediated by group symbols. . . . It is symbolic communication that makes it possible for the group to attend to its own behavior; and language which enables the group to do this with greater precision. Language makes it possible for the group to symbolize its own group mind, and so gives group mind the power of becoming conscious group mind.[25]

Of importance here is the double-moment of "group mind" articulated through language as ideology. On the one hand, shared language and symbols provide an identity for the group. Ideology thereby contributes to the definition of "we/they."[26] On the other hand, this identity is put forward in a "non-antagonistic" fashion with respect to other groups.

A moment's thought shows this "non-antagonism" to be no small feat in the context of a modern industrial society. As developed in what follows, antagonism pervades the institutions of this social order, institutions which divide society into classes and groups and which allocate differential rewards, privileges and positions of power. Such institutions tend to generate motives for action which are incongruent with social norms arrived at through free and open discussion, arrived at, in other words, through that to which all modern industrial societies lay claim—"democracy." Inasmuch as ideology tends to symbolically disguise the motives for social action, it simultaneously tends to conceal from the conscious inspection of both the group itself and outsiders the institutions which structure the action. Thus, incongruity is turned into its opposite; the *motives* for action are obscured while society is integrated around the *consequences*, symbolically represented, of the action itself.[27] Examples of such are not hard to come by. Take, for instance, the construction of a convention center by a municipality in the US. Commonly, construction interests, motivated by private gain, are among the prime movers in bringing about public expenditures for private purposes (e.g., business conventions). Other social groups, however, are "integrated around the consequences" of these projects with appeals such as "This will mean jobs for our city."

In summary, then, ideology can be seen as ideational cement for the *status quo*. This "function," as it were, can be traced through a series of contradictions which locate ideology within its social context. This context is, of course, a contradictory social order, a class society. Ideology incorporates the contradictions of this social order and transforms them into natural events, inevitable conditions and impersonal processes, thus explaining, justifying and stabilizing real conditions of domination before the dominators and the dominated alike. Yet this movement of social contradictions from social practice to ideological thought in no way expunges the contradictions themselves. These reappear within ideology as the parallel development of argumentative reason and irrational symbology. Murray Edelman, who has pioneered the study of political symbols in contemporary American political science, argues that any culture commonly contains mutually exclusive explanations for a given event, something which "makes possible a wide spectrum of ambivalent postures for each individual and a similarly large set of contradictions in political rhetoric and in public policy."[28] Likewise, through the medium of ideology, individuals have access simultaneously to rational-argumentative and mythic-symbolic modes of cognition and explanation. The presence of each might serve as an identifying characteristic of ideological thought; i.e., these modes come into contradiction with one another and such contradictions can be spotted with critical reading. More importantly, however, the combination of elements drawn from these conflicting sources provide ideology with its particular force, its ability to speak with reason's voice and yet utter a word magic which carries its explanations far beyond reason's finite domain. This ambivalence is, finally, of no small import with respect to providing a focus of identity for the class or social group which spawns the ideology and other classes or groups from which it seeks legitimation. With particular reference to administrators, the focus of this study, Edelman's work is again instructive:

. . . ambiguity in definition and in perception is a major source of bureaucratic power and discretion, and it complements a related ambiguity as to when administrators solve and when they aggravate the problems with which they are supposed to cope.[29]

Such ambiguity in administrative ideology enables the group in question to integrate others around the products of administrative action by wrapping these products in the sort of symbols which secure their acceptance and, concomitantly, legitimate the bureaucratic order itself.

A Method of Analysis

Our discussion of the concept of ideology has already adumbrated, at least indirectly, some methodological guidelines for analyzing the phenomenon of ideology: a critical perspective, an interpretive approach and a sense of ideology's social bases. These flow from the meaning of the concept so far developed. Here we might extend this discussion by outlining a *method* of analysis which corresponds to our *object* of analysis, ideology. This method might be called "historical-critical."

The first dimension of this method, that of history, connotes an appreciation of "totality," i.e., a sustained effort to situate ideology within its social context and to grasp it as part of that context.[30] Ideology and its social basis develop in tandem and over time. What is more, ideology reflects its bases in the social world, but in a partial or one-sided manner. Consequently, in speaking of ideologies today, it is not enough simply to list the elements of such and to show how these relate to actual behavior. Some understanding of history, not only "what was" but, in a sense, "what might have been," is crucial in explaining both the content of an ideology and the role which the ideology plays in the world.[31] Similarly, explanation of contemporary conditions in terms of their historical development cannot content itself with "mere" history. The effort, as C. Wright Mills[32] argued, must always be directed toward showing how the past is sustained within the present. In this respect, it may not be amiss to think of social institutions, which engirdle human action and give it a particular coherence, predictability and meaning, as sustainers of the past. Ideology can then be counted as the naturalization of these institutions and their history.

Inasmuch as ideology refashions in thought its bases in social practice, a critical method is required to ferret out the linkage between the two, and to understand each as conditioned by the other. In this respect, both ideology and the social conditions which it reflects are *appearances,* as it were, what might be taken as "the given." A critical approach explores the relations between them and treats these *relations* as the reality manifested in each.[32] It falls to critical thinking, in the words of Juergen Habermas, to ask:

What lies behind the consensus, presented as a fact, that supports the dominant tradition of the time, and [critical thinking] does so with a view to the relations of power surreptitiously incorporated in the symbolic structures of speech and action. The immunizing power of ideologies, which stifle demands for justification raised by discursive examination, goes back to blockages in communication, independently of the changing semantic contents.[33]

Critically examined, ideology is something of a set of clues to "what lies behind the consensus," i.e., to the relation between the material conditions of social life and the manner in which these appear in ideology.

A critical approach sheds fresh light on the problem of objectivity, i.e., the objection that might be raised to the effect that the analyst of ideology is perforce contaminated with the very malady which he is examining and is, therefore, incapable of arriving at an "objective" point of view. The viewpoint of critique, to follow Habermas again, "cannot simply stop at the contradiction between subjectivity and the reified world," rather "it confronts limited life with this life's own concept."[34] Objectivity cannot be taken as a state of being. Rather, it is always a process of becoming whereby we penetrate and go beyond the false-objectivity of appearances and begin to see these in their relational aspect. Objectivity, then, presupposes critique.

Finally, I would like to mention two principles associated with the phenomenological tradition which seem to me invaluable for the analysis of ideology: "understanding" and "intentionality." These supplement the method and suggest some techniques for deploying it. The concept of understanding, which we have already met in passing, calls on the student of society to recreate the social world of those whom he studies, to reach an empathetic appreciation of their behavior by understanding their world as they see it.[35] I am convinced that such understanding is indispensable to the enterprise of critique, but I am equally persuaded that criticism is essential to full understanding.[36] This seems a contradiction, combining empathy and criticism in the same method. However, it is within this very contradiction or tension that the strength of the method lies; i.e., it makes possible a deeper comprehension of the object by going beyond its immediate appearance. It does so by asking, basically, two questions: What did the social actors (the "object" of investigation) believe themselves to be doing? And, What were they really doing? Neither question is answerable without recourse to the other. An answer emerges as a sort of dialectic between them. Here, empathy adds to explanation the dimension of subjective motivation, without which any objective appraisal of events is perforce incomplete and, hence, something less than objective. Criticism contributes the element of objective determination, the suspicion, as it were, that no matter what men thought themselves to be doing, there was more to it than that; there were social forces at play, of which the actors may or may not have been conscious. These forces operate, in a sense, independently of the subjective views of the actors and, to some extent, help to shape these views themselves.[37] What present themselves as apparently contradictory sides of this formulation of the concept, understanding, can now be seen as mutually-constituting, complementary dimensions of a single method aimed at preserving the qualitative concreteness of the object of study and explaining it by drawing out what Karl Mannheim has called the "interconnections between social situations on the one hand and psychic-ethical modes of behavior on the other."[38]

The principle of intentionality is related to understanding as a method of inquiry. Intentionality posits an active ingredient in the human subject and a reciprocal object for human activity. This is to say that were we to speak of the intentional nature of consciousness, for instance, we would mean that consciousness is always consciousness of something, or knowledge—always knowledge of something—and so on.[39] The importance of intentionality for present purposes is two-fold. First, it sensitizes us to the mutual inter-relation between man and his world, a concern which springs from the method of understanding, but which finds a sharper, more precise expression within the idea of intentionality. Second, the principle of intentionality provides a conceptual grounding for the technique of imputation, one of the primary tools of analysis in the present study.

Imputation, as explained by Mannheim, is a technique whereby the analyst seeks the perspective imbedded within the individual ideas under examination and brings "the perspective thus established into relationship with the currents of thought of which it is a part. These currents of thought, in turn must be traced back to the social forces determining them."[40] Implicit here is the assumption that the world of ideas, far from being a random jumble of isolated outlooks, is a social world where coherency in outlook obtains within perspectives or within larger currents. Such coherency is a product of the interconnection of thought and life as intentionality might suggest. Imputation endeavors to uncover this interconnection; according to Mannheim, it does so on two levels:

The first deals with general problems of interpretation. It reconstructs integral styles of thought and perspectives, tracing single expressions and records of thought which appear to be related to a central *Weltanschauung*, which they express. It makes explicit the whole of a system which is implicit in the discrete segments of a system of thought. . . .

The second level of imputation operates by assuming that the ideal types built up through the process above described are indispensable hypotheses for research, and then asking to what extent . . . in individual cases, these ideal-types were actually realized in their thinking.[41]

Finally, the analyst attempts to explain the forms and variations in thought by deriving them "from the composition of the groups and strata which express themselves in that mode of thought."[42]

The application of the historical-critical method, and, in particular, the technique of imputation, to the ideology of administration includes the following steps. We begin by turning to the professional literature on administrative in the US and the USSR, in order to reconstruct administration's self-understanding. Here the analysis is concerned to investigate at the most general level consistent patterns of thought which address the nature of administration and establish its raison d'etre. This reconstruction derived from the highly articulated expressions of administrative thought yields an ideal-type of administrative ideology consonant with the first level of imputation. It is called "administrative rationality" and can be taken as the general ideology of administration. Bringing the ideology at this level into critical focus, administrative rationality is measured against administrative practice. In so doing, contradictions surface within the general ideology and within the practice which generates it and which is in turn guided by the ideology. These contradictions seek resolution, and ideology of administrative obliges in the form of what are called "special ideologies of administration," each directed toward symbolically surmounting the contradictions in thought and practice at the general level.

The special ideologies of administration are charted in the second part of this study. The effort is always to show how and why these come about by tracing their roots back to a contradictory practice which is ideologically legitimated. Data gathered from interviews with American and Soviet administrators and from those who educate and train them advances the analysis to the second level of imputation. At this stage the intention is to ground empirically the ideal-types already developed and to uncover variations in administrative ideology which relates to the particular positions and practices of those in the interview sample.

2
Modern Industrialism and the Phenomenon of Bureaucracy

The ideology of administration, like any other, is an aspect of a totality. That is, it is the expression in thought of the conditions under which men reproduce themselves in the social world and the relations which they form with one another in the process of doing so. This much follows from the foregoing critique of the conventional concept of "bureaucratic ideology" and the attempt to situate the concept upon a sounder basis, both theoretically and methodologically. Our purposes in this chapter are to set out some general comments on the other aspects of this totality (namely, the mode of reproduction and the corresponding social relations) and to draw out the connections between these and the ideological form in which they are expressed.

"Modern Industrialism" is a concept which embraces societies as manifestly dissimilar as the United States and the Soviet Union. The very breadth of such a concept would seem to invite a host of problems. How can we compare, to take only a few examples, a society in which the bulk of economic power is in private hands and rests ultimately on the institution of the market with one in which no market exists and the economy is owned and directed by the state? Or a society in which the top political leadership is recruited through the medium of competitive elections with one in which a single party exists and supplies all the leadership positions? Or the independent groups, so common in American politics, with the formal prohibition against the same which obtains in the Soviet Union? These are real differences and must be recognized as such. Yet the concept of modern industrialism holds the promise of a "deeper" similarity between its late capitalist and nominally socialist variants, a similarity which we might at this point explore by marking out the three axes on which the concept turns: technology, human organization and ideology.

Technological Determination

A common conception of technology in modern industrial society (a conception, which, to anticipate ourselves a bit, is central to the ideology of administration) portrays technology as the socially neutral ensemble of machines, processes, techniques, skills and so forth which determine the range of organizational forms available to men.[1] Those technologies which are superior from the point of view of productivity are, and will be, introduced. Technological change, then, accounts for the rise and fall of organizational forms. With the advent of the assembly line in automotive production, to take a familiar example, the scale of operations, the task structure and the organizational hierarchy were all radically altered. Older forms of organization, rooted in the industry's ancestry, carriage manufacture, soon disappeared either because firms did not keep pace with the technological change and were unable to compete effectively or because they adopted themselves this technological innovation begun at Ford.[2]

Technology, doubtless, does determine the forms of human organization. But technology neither falls from the sky nor emerges from beneath a rock. Its origin is, of course, in society, and by viewing technology as a social institution we can locate its determination in the relations among men, in the specific social formations within which given technologies arise and develop. Some recent work employing this perspective has found that technological innovation follows a course charted by the dominant class in society. In the era of capitalism, for instance, we need to look no further than the advent of the factory system which *predated* industrialism proper and the specialization of functions based on machine technology. The factory system, an arrangement which permitted the supervision of the many (the producers) by the few (the owners), represented a response to the problem of insuring maximum productivity within a setting in which labor was alienated from its product. It was into this system that large scale machine technology was introduced; technology which, doubtless, increased productivity, but, more importantly for present purposes, one which expressed in a technical form, as a technical necessity, the same regimentation and hierarchy which were already features of the factory system itself.[3]

The claim that technology is determined by class relations can be read in two ways. On the one hand, it refers to various segments of the ruling class actively seeking out and promoting those technical innovations which contribute to their form of rule. For capitalist society such amounts to technical changes which enhance the control of the ruling class over society's surplus product, or, what is essentially the same thing, those which increase the profits of the relevant capitalist by lowering their costs of production and increasing their share of the market. The history of technical innovation in the modern era, from the steam engine[4] to the solar power tower,[5] is replete with instances of such consciously directed action by members of the capitalist class.[6]

On the other hand, the forms taken by technology can be seen as determined by less personal, but no less social, processes. From this perspective, technical change is an outcome of class relations and, most particularly, of class struggle. Here, the category of structural limitation is a useful one for understanding the range and variations in technological innovation. Structured limitation connotes a certain coherence and interdependence among society's ideological, political and economic structures. More specifically:

[it] constitutes a pattern of determination in which some social structure establishes limits within which some other structure or process can vary and establishes probabilities for the specific structures or processes that are possible within those limits. That is, structural limitation implies that certain forms of the determined structure have been excluded entirely and some possible forms are more likely than others.[8]

Applying this idea to capitalist society and its technology, an aspect of the economic structure, we can note a tendency for technical innovations to follow a path which is consonant with the maintenance and reproduction of other structures in capitalist society. Such technical innovations, however, have not occurred as a mere unilateral imposition on the part of the capitalist class. Rather, as Irwin Yellowitz has shown, they have met sustained, albeit largely unsuccessful, resistance from workers.[9] In this respect, technical change can be grasped as an outcome of class struggle.

The Bases of Bureaucracy

Changes in the form of human organization too can be understood as products of class struggle. To the degree that organizational forms are adapted to innovations in the technological infrastructure, this is already obvious. What is more, however, organizations in class society reflect in their interior the struggle among classes. Each organization is a task structure, but equally each is simultaneously a conflict system wherein control over the work process is the primary issue in the contest among groups within the organization.[10] Richard Edwards has documented for a number of large American organizations the internal struggle over this "contested terrain," and has demonstrated how organizational forms evolve as solutions to management's problem of control over the work force and the work process. Each "solution," far from removing the internal conflict, instead transfers it to other quarters and alters both the concrete issues in the contest and the capacity of each side to continue the struggle within the new organization framework which has evolved.[11]

Two dimensions of the concept "modern industrial society," as formulated by Raymond Aron, represent the basic contours of this contested terrain. These are "the technological division of labor within the firm" and "economic calculation."[12] In part, "economic calculation" refers to the rationale for the introduction of modern industrial technology. From this point of view, technology which lowers the cost of producing a given commodity meets the criterion of economic calculation or, what is the same thing, "economic rationality." This criterion merits discussion in its own right and, consequently, we shall return to it shortly. What is important here is what "stand between," so to speak, the technology on the one hand, and the normative criterion ("economic rationality") on the other. This "middle term" is people engaged in the social act of production. What sort of technology and what attendant relationships among the producers is in accord with the dictates of economic rationality? Here again we can be brief. Technology which utilizes a maximum of unskilled and, therefore, cheap labor which is organized along a bureaucratic pattern.

The word "bureaucracy" has a special significance in this context. Although bureaucratic forms predated industrialism, it is only with the advent of capitalism (commodity production, money economy) as Max Weber recognized,[13] that the bureaucratic form became the prevailing

mode of social organization. The economic dynamic ("economic rationality") responsible for the growth of bureaucracy—technological innovations utilizing cheap labor and resulting in increased profit for the
owners—expressed itself as the progressive separation of conception
from execution in the process of production, the widening gap between the purpose of human behavior and that behavior itself. This is
what Aron means by the "technological division of labor within the
firm." Harry Braverman has, I think, more concisely captured the
essence of this phenomenon with the phrase " the subdivision of labor
in detail."[14] Modern industrialism goes beyond a simple division of
labor; rather, it decomposes each task (and each skill) into so many
isolated and reptitious operations. As the number of discrete operations proliferates, so grows the need to coordinate and control those
performing them. This need is met through the creation of new organizational layers whose task is supervisory. Knowledge of the productive
process adheres in these supervisory layers and increases as one moves
up the organizational hierarchy such that "the whole" is only compre-
hensible at "the top." At the bottom, at the level of actual performance
or execution, no knowledge or skill is required beyond that which
pertains to the immediate, segmented and routinized task.[15]

Marx used the term "human labor in the abstract" (or "human labor
in general")[16] to connote a mass of producers, stripped of *qualitative*
skills and reduced to a pure *quantity* of labor;[17] Weber, the expression
"domination structure," to describe the totality of relations among
these "labor quantities" in the bureaucratic apparatus.[18] Each of these
characterizations represents the complement of the other. The relations
among "labor quantities" are expressed in "a social structure which is
ordered hierarchy according to materialistic achievement norms, has
objectified labor so that there is a high degree of (not necessarily and
not usually vertical) social mobility, and is disciplined by the regulariza-
tion of activity in quantified time."[19] As Raymond Aron has shown,
these features are the hallmarks of modern industrial society and are
common to either its Western capitalist or Soviet "socialist" variants. In
either setting, man as "labor quantity" is simply another word for man
qua instrument of production, commodity, object, thing.[20] Considered
from this viewpoint, bureaucracy is the mechanism through which the
isolated and segmented activities of these human "things" which pop-
ulate it are harnessed to attain the objectives of those who command
the bureaucratic machine

This economic dynamic propelling the growth of bureaucracy (the reduction of human labor to quantity and its attendant subdivision into discrete, routinized operations) is supplemented by a social one. Claude Lefort has put it thusly:

> The status of the bureaucrat is measured by the number of secretaries and employees who depend on him, by the number of telephones and machines at his service, more generally, by the authority allocated to his domain of organization. . . . The more activities are fragmented, services diversified, specialized and partitioned, the more numerous the structural levels and the delegations of authority at each level, the more coordination and control sectors multiply because of this dispersion. Thus the bureaucracy prospers. [21]

To the view of bureaucracy as the reflection of "objective" needs in human organization (the needs for supervision, coordination, planning), the concept of bureaucracy as a social system adds an understanding of the "subjective" side of this phenomenon. It alerts us to the fact that the neatly drawn lines on an organizational chart are to some extent an idealization of the relations among *real* people operating within an organizational hierarchy. To the degree that bureaucratically structured organizations depend on large numbers of employees whose work is not directly productive (e.g. supervisors and inspectors), the organizational form taken by such "surplus labor power," to follow Adam Przeworski's analysis, is itself directly determined by class struggle,[22] which continues within the organization as a contest over power and position.[23]

This two-fold struggle over the form of organized human activity and over respective positions and power of those within a given organization need not and should not be interpreted as implying a continuous, conscious collective effort at overthrowing, from below, the "domination structure" or, for that matter, of actively attending and reinforcing, from above, the patterns of organizational authority. To be sure, the struggle does take such forms, albeit rarely. On an everyday basis, however, we are much more likely to encounter other manifestations of conflict. Workers, for instance, "hold back" their labor; they work more slowly and less diligently than they might, they find a store room in which to hide from their supervisors, they phone in "sick" and thus temporarily withdraw from the labor process altogether. The point is that even such relatively passive actions are manifestations of the struggle among classes as it is played out between workers and their superiors within bureaucratic organizations.[24] The ideology of administration is itself rooted in this struggle and much of it, especially its operational techniques, can be counted as weapons forged for the fight and collected in what Soviet writers so straightforwardly call "the arsenal of the administrative leader."[25] In order to understand the nature of such weapons and the manner in which they are deployed, we turn now to the general outlines of administrative ideology.

Rationality and Bureaucracy: The General Outlines of Administrative Ideology

The Transformation of the Concept "Rationality" in the Modern World

The concept of "rationality" has deep roots in the Western philosophic tradition. These we need bear in mind as we simultaneously disassociate the modern meaning of "rational" from its historical relevance.[26] The idea of rationality is no more immune to myth than is any other and although the concept can be formulated rather precisely in its modern form, it also exists as a symbol and, therefore, draws on a myriad of historical-philosophical associations which provide it with a connotative richness embedded in the Western tradition.[27]

In the modern world, rationality has become a consideration which applies to means, never to ends. Weber was perhaps the first to articulate this. He used the term *zweckrational* to refer to the act of "making use of these expectations (concerning the behavior of others or that of physical objects) as 'conditions' or 'means' for the successful attainment of the actor's own rationally chosen ends."[28] The phrase "rationally chosen ends" does not mean an objective, selected by reason, and valued for its own sake. For such an end, Weber employed the word *wertrational*. Rather, in the case of *zweckrational*, "the ends, the means, and the secondary results are all taken rationally into account and weighed."[29] Ends *per se* are not subject to the scrutiny of reason. They are compared one with another and with the respective means to them within the framework of "marginal utility" where "absolute values are always irrational."[30]

The modern notion of rationality, then, has shed the traditional rationalist preoccupation with ends themselves, absolute values or ultimate purposes. Insofar as ends are an object of rational consideration, they are not something standing apart from or above the means. Their status is a contingent one, depending on the means; questions of ends are, thereby, reduced to question of means.[31] In C. Wright Mills' apt expression, modern rationality is a "rationality without reason."[32]

The Rationality of Science

The above characterization of rationality in its modern form is traceable to the scientific revolution of the seventeenth century,[33] i.e., to the scientific mode of knowing which replaced considerations of quality with those of quantity, which conceived of its object, nature, as quantifiable "stuff" which cannot only be known through mathematized relations, but, given this mode of knowing, manipulated and, ultimately, dominated by man.[34] The purpose or ends of such manipulation are foreign to scientific thought. These involve values and, as such, can only be supplied from without, that is, by society.

In the application of scientific knowledge through the medium of technology,[35] purposes or ends are present, yet are, so to speak, hidden within the technological apparatus. This much would follow from the remarks registered above on the social determination of technology, the manner in which technology incorporates the social relations of dominance within its technical form. Here, Aron's comments have a special meaning:

The object of every industrial society is to asert the power of man over nature (of which the power of some men over others is an unavoidable consequence).

The domination of nature implies the domination of "some men over others,"as Leiss in particular has shown,[37] because the appropriation of nature for human purposes occurs within a class society, and the technology and organizational forms by means of which such appropriation occurs are stamped with the mark of that society and its class structure.

Technical Rationality as the Logic of Bureaucracy

The term "technical rationality" is a derivative of the rationality of modern science. Like science, it is a mode of thought which converts quality into quantity. Like science, it cannot address itself, at least directly, to questions of ends or values. However, it *does not share* with science the character of being apart from the affairs of men in society, of proceeding according to its own inner rules.[38] On the contrary, technical rationality, as a mode of thought, can be understood as an expression of power relations in the social world, on the one hand, and as a mystification of those relations on the other. It represents "the purposeful organization and combination of productive techniques"[39] and, from this viewpoint, appears as "neutral," as the rational adaptation of means to ends (whatever these may be). Such "organization and combination," however, occur within a given social formation which is anything but "neutral," which is characterized by a impersonal form of domination which is, as we have seen, built into the "productive techniques" themselves. As a mode of thought oblivious to these real relations of dominance, taking the world and its ends as "given," technical rationality transforms the conditions of domination in society from a political category into a technical one. For this reason, it can be counted as an ideology *par excellence.* More precisely, it is the general ideology of bureaucracy.

What is the relation then, between bureaucracy, a form of organization and technical rationality, a way of thinking or apprehending the world? As Weber pointed out, each finds its historical source point in capitalism, a society based on the institution of the market in which the relationships among people and things become quantified (in the form of money) and take on a non-human form (or, what is the same thing, are devoid of all qualitative characteristics) and as a result are subject to rational calculation (money providing the indispensible standard equivalent for all things in the market).[40] We have discussed, above, the genesis of modern bureaucracy within this setting and have noted the growth of bureaucratic structures as a consequence of the subdivision of labor in detail and the concomitant divorce of conception or control from execution. It remains here to specify how such relationships, through the medium of technical rationality, present themselves to actors in the social world.

The defining element of relations inside a bureaucracy is *hierarchy*, itself another word for domination. Given the world-view of technical rationality, however, bureaucracy does not appear as a structure of domination; on the contrary, the bureaucratic hierarchy manifests itself as a technical necessity (to coordinate the subdivided tasks), as a rational organizational arrangement for the accomplishment of collective ends.[41] We can say, then, with Habermas that "in accordance with this rationality, the institutionalization of the conditions of life is synonymous with the institutionalization of a form of domination whose political character becomes unrecognizable."[42]

The word "unrecognizable" in this passage is of crucial importance. It is brought into sharp relief by two additional comments which Habermas has made:

The thought that the relations of production can be measured against the potential of developed productive forces is prevented because the existing relations of production present themselves as the technically necessary organizational form for a rationalized society.[43]

And, with special reference to the United States and the Soviet Union:

The assertion that politically consequential decisions are reduced to carrying out the immanent exigencies of disposable techniques and that therefore they can no longer be made the theme of practical considerations, serves in the end merely to conceal pre-existing, unreflected social interests and prescientific decisions.[44]

Technical rationality, as a logic of political control, evinces two counter-balancing movements. On the one hand, social interests and the attendant political claims appear in the guise of technical necessity. On the other, the objects of such political control, given the form of control itself (technical necessity), are unable to constitute themselves as political subjects by challenging the system which renders them as objects. To challenge is to negate, and negating the "rational" is "irrational," just as challenging the "necessary" is "unnecessary."[45]

This double movement of the ideology in the social consciousness reproduces itself in a double sense through the actions of bureaucracy and the comprehension of such actions through the medium of ideology. That is, technical rationality is instrumental thinking;[46] it leads to courses of action, techniques of organization, and so forth, which "get things done." This is its *effective* side, to which corresponds simultaneously, as part of the same course of action, the same organizational technique, and so on, an *affective* side which offers legitimations for administrative actions and for the results of such. There is no better illustration of this double movement than the cult of expertise; the notion that social decisions are far too complicated and important to be trusted to society—rather, they must be made by those who possess the requisite competence, i.e., the administrative expert. As we shall see in succeeding chapters, the cult of expertise is not confined to claims of competence. Rather, to the proposition "only the qualified can decide," it adds "only the qualified should decide." And this "should" is based on a self-perception which highlights the supposed moral altruism of modern administration and modern administrators.

Already this analysis contradicts the conclusions of two thinkers from whom I have learned much on the subject of ideology and administration, namely, Habermas and Joyce A. Hertzler. Habermas holds that modern industrial societies face a "legitimation crisis" precisely because "traditions important for legitimation cannot be regenerated administratively."[47] As more of life is subsumed under administrative rules, as life becomes "administered life" (to use the expression of the Frankfurt School), meaning, motivation and society's normative structure erode. It is not clear what consequences (e.g., a drift toward anomie, a resurgence of messianic movements) this portends, but there is no doubt for Habermas that the rationalization of society through the medium of administration has inaugurated a deep and permanent state of crisis in modern industrial societies. What Habermas overlooks, however, is that there is no *a priori* reason to suppose that the irrational, legitimating myths of tradition cannot be combined with rational, calculated action on the part of power-holders.[48] The degree to which such combinations are internally contradictory or, owing to their more or less conscious manufacture, relatively transparent, is a question which can only be answered empirically.

Hertzler recognizes that the language of administration "is above all the language of the governing techniques of the organization; it is primarily concerned with the exercise of authority,"[49] the use of *legitimate* power. Consequently, she argues that administrative language contains both an unequivocal/operational element and symbolic side which legitimizes the former.[50] These she treats as discrete dimensions of administrative language, but, in so doing, misses the possibility that the unequivocal element *can* exist as a symbolic justification itself as our discussion of rationality (e.g., the command is presented as a "rational" one) might sugguest.

We might interpret, then, technical rationality as the general ideology of administration; "general" in that it is not peculiar to administrators themselves (it clearly pertains to the larger social ideology of "scientism"[51]) but is the overriding ethos of modern administration all the same. In unravelling further the dialectics of this general ideology in the following chapter, we shall locate contradictions at the general level which generate in their turn special ideologies of administration, each a confluence of effective and affective currents within the mainstream of administrative thought. And within this confluence some rather extraordinary things happen to the currents themselves. Not only do they merge into a single flow, each inextricable from the other, but their very union results in two corollary inversions. These are: the glorification of the trivial and the trivialization of the sublime or important. The thrust of administrative thought in the United States and the Soviet Union is to turn the ordinary humdrum of everyday routine into wondrous events by portraying this routine as "building communism" or "self-actualization." Conversely, ideas which are important, which in some way constitute a challenge to the existing order (say "communism," "democracy" or "self-actualization"), are emasculated and metamorphosed into anthems of administrative rule.

Variants of Modern Industrialism: The United States and the Soviet Union

Having anchored our analysis of bureaucracy in the dynamics of a capitalist economy, the reader may well be wondering about the relevance of such to "socialist," or at least "non-capitalist," countries like the Soviet Union. We shall address this issue here in terms of three aspects of modern industrialism which bear directly on the ideology of administration and its bases in the social order: the constitution of society's "governing class," the structure of relations within bureaucratic organizations and the nature of political relations within a modern industrial society. In so doing, we shall treat the US as something of a standard against which the Soviet experience might be compared. Although the purpose in this approach is heuristic, we might also note in passing that from Lenin onward the Soviets have viewed the American industrial order as a model for themselves and have borrowed liberally from it.[52]

We have already noted that an explanation of administrative ideology depends on tracing the forms taken by administrative thought back to their bases in social practice. We can do no more here, however, than to sketch out those aspects of the modern industrial order which are most germane to our interest, relying on citations to indicate where a more complete development of the argument might be found. Obviously, even an abstract or general discussion of the emergence of modern industrialism in its American and Soviet versions is far too large a task to be adequately, let alone exhaustively, dealt with within the scope of this study. Yet, in keeping with our method, some, however incomplete, treatment of this subject is indispensable in order to bring the ideology of administration into proper focus.

Constitution of the Governing Class

In *Politics and Markets*, Charles E. Lindblom advances the intriguing thesis that by tracing out the fundamental dynamics at play in countries such as the United States and the Soviet Union, each organized on different structural principles (the market for the former, the plan for the latter), we discover that each in certain respects seems to turn into the other.[53] For instance, Lindblom points out that the appearance of rational planning in the USSR belies a situation in which economic calculation, a precondition of such planning, does not properly exist, owing to the absence of a market and a price system reflecting real costs. Conversely, in a market system such as the US, we find that extensive and effective economic planning occurs within large corporations. Most importantly for our purposes, Lindblom notes that everday life for most people in these societies looks quite the same,i.e., it takes place within large hierarchically ordered organizations and is subject to the apparently impersonal discipline of these institutions. Further, enormous differences on the surface of political life reveal on inspection an overriding similarity, viz., the use of political power has passed into the hands of those who command these large bureaucratic organizations. Lindblom is keenly aware, as are other writers on this subject,[54] that this usage of political power is not an unfettered one; it transpires within the ambit and under the constraints of society's fundamental institution or organizing principle—the market or the plan. Consequently, we can analytically distinguish between administrators, a governing class,[55] and those who by reason of their privileged positions within the social order appropriate and determine the use of society's surplus product, that is, those who constitute a ruling class.[56] In drawing this distinction, we recognize that empirically there is a considerable overlap in membership between the governing and ruling classes of either country. Moreover, it follows that the function or act of ruling within a modern industrial society is a mediated one, ocurring through the medium of administration.

With respect to the development of the American political economy in this century, two generalizations are immediately possible: (a) economic activity has been concentrated in progressively larger units,[57] and (b) there has been a concomitant growth in the size and scope of the state with an attendant interdependence and inter-penetration obtaining between state and economy.[58] Taken together, these aspects of the American political economy have been addressed under the theoretical rubrics of "(state) monopoly capitalism"[59] and "late" or "neo"-capitalism.[60] Government by administration is the hallmark of the political order in either instance and despite certain exaggerations and some important lapses (especially with regard to the institution of property in late capitalist society), John Burnham[61] and John Kenneth Galbraith[62] were right in drawing our attention to this seminal fact. As a governing class, administrators experience directly, we might conclude, the tensions or contradictions of the social order. And, as we shall see below, it is these contradictions which give impetus and shape to the ideology of administration.

Turning to the Soviet Union, we can say without reservation that comparable theoretical work elucidating the fundamental structures and "laws of motion" (to use the Marxian expression) of that society does not at this time exist. It is only within the past decade that the study of the USSR, long the province of purely descriptive and often polemical work,[63] has graduated to the level of theoretical investigation. What theoretical work does exist at this time remains provisional, incomplete and tendentious. Nonetheless, some advances have been made and we might draw upon these in outling the position of the Soviet Union's governing class.

Theoretical analyses which approach the Soviet Union as a historically unique social formation, one which is neither capitalist nor socialist, seem to me to be on the strongest footing. Here, the work of

Antonio Carlo[64] and Hillel Ticktin[65] merits particular attention. Soviet society, in the view of each, contains certain traces of a class structure, but these are not fully articulated because of the mechanism by which the surplus product is appropriated. Whereas private property and the market under capitalism mean that the surplus is realized by a class of people *individually* (capitalists), accumulation and disposition of the surplus product in the Soviet context occurs through the institutions of state property and the plan, that is, by a class (or group) of people *collectively*. Consequently, Carlo uses the expression "bureaucratic collectivism" and Ticktin the term "elite" to designate what I take to be the Soviet ruling class. Owing to its constitution through state property and the plan some important distinctions follow for this class and its method of rule. First, the privileged position which its members hold in society is closely bound up in most cases with governing. Although the social privilege evident in the higher circles of the USSR includes a contingent of favored artists, performers, academicians and so on, the overwhelming percentage of the ruling class derive their privilege from the office which they hold. They are, in the main, administrators who participate directly in governing. Second, the mechanism of rule, unlike the capitalist market, is in the Soviet instance directly political. As Rainer Paris has pointed out, class domination of this sort is an unstable one, one which needs to be more or less constantly and consciously attended. As a result, overt coercion and the censorship have become the principal means for effecting class rule, along with large dosages of preposterous propaganda, the ubiquity of which produces and "illusory politicization of the public sphere" while its real aim is quite the opposite, "the effective depoliticization of the masses."[66] These circumstances lend to Soviet administrative ideology a number of shades and tones not found on the American side. Third, the generation and appropriation of the surplus under Soviet conditions is itself an unstable and imperfect process. With no market, neither are prices subject to rational calculations, nor is the working population disciplined by the threat of unemployment. The upshot seems to be that enterprise directors, in their own interest, continually deceive the planners, while employees, in their own interest, are able to offer sustained resistance (taking the form of negotiated labor norms, low productivity, shoddy work and absenteeism) to enterprise directors.[67] Again, these conditions leave their peculiar mark on administrative ideology in the USSR.

The Structure of Relations Within Bureaucratic Organizations

In the United States, the origins of modern administration are trace-able to organizational innovations designed to accomodate the increas-ing size and diversity of operations in certain large businesses. Specifically, as Alfred D. Chandler, Jr., has shown, these innovations involved the creation of a central board of executives within the firm which is freed from the everyday exigencies of management and is able, therefore, to concern itself with the more comprehensive tasks of policy making and planning.[68] The productive work, carried out at lower levels of the organizational hierarchy and entrusted to the direc-tion of salaried professionals, has become more and more routinized and devoid of craft skills as we have already noted. Here, we might emphasize that the de-skilling of occupations, in addition to being a cost-saving device which lowers the wage rate, also plays a principal role in organizational strategies designed to increase managerial con-trol over the work force. That is, the standardization of parts and processes in the large industrial firm was quickly followed by an equivalent standardization and interchangeability of the "human parts" of the organization.[69] As Alvin Gouldner,[70] among others,[71] has demonstrated, work and a work force organized on such lines takes control of the work process out of the hands of those who perform it and lodges this control in management. Control of the work process is, of course, only another name for control of the human parts of the process itself. Such control, more or less perfected, has never become complete. That is, the objects of these structural innovations, workers, have under varying conditions and to varying degrees recognized an interest of their own independent of the organization as represented by top administration. The ensuing contest of interests has imprinted on modern organizations an abiding character of two camps or two poles of interest and allegiance: that of the formal organization and that of an informal workers' subculture.[72] In the dynamics of this conflict we shall locate in succeeding chapters a primary source of administrative ideol-ogy.

There are some striking parallels to these developments in the Soviet experience. First, we might note the wholesale adoption of the capital-ist technology and Western, particularly American, organizational methods immediately after the October Revolution.[73] Implicit in the Bolshevik thinking of this time was the idea that the same machine which accounts for exploitation, alienation and a host of other social ills common to capitalism can, provided that the machine is directed by the right people, transport humanity to the good society.[74] "Socialism," Lenin wrote shortly after the Revolution, "is merely the next step forward from state-capitalist monopoly. Or, in other words, socialism is merely state-capitalist monopoly *which is made to serve the interest of the whole people* and has to that *extent* ceased to be capitalist monopoly."[75] We find, in short, the imposition of many of the features of the organizational forms developed under capitalism as a key element in the Bolshevik design of the new Soviet state. The emerging forms of workers' democracy which had in many instances made rapid advances under the revolutionary conditions which prevailed in Russia were, accordingly, jettisoned.[76] No more than a few months, for example, after the October Revolution, we find Lenin, confronted with an upsurge of spontaneous activity from among workers demanding direct control over their factories, remarking:

Large scale industry—which is the material productive force and foundation of socialism—calls for absolute and strict unity of will. . . . How can strict unity of will be ensured? By thousands subordinating their wills to the will of one.[77]

The control of the work force under Soviet circumstances differs from the American case only in detail. That is, the hierarchical structure of the organization and the basic design of the work process are quite similar. Differences, it seems to me, center on the absence of a labor market in the USSR and the attendant lack of control through the threat of unemployment. To some degree this has been compensated for by the regimen of the work book (a full record of a worker's employment history which is a document all must possess), differential access to such things as housing and vacationing, and the rather direct mechanism of the production campaign, "socialist competition" and "emulation." As we shall see below, these differences in the form of control carry over into the forms taken by administrative ideology; namely, in the United States where an impersonal institution, the labor market, enforces discipline and promotes competition these matters are not addressed as often or as urgently as they are in the Soviet Union where such discipline and competition are consciously induced and constantly attended.

Political Relations in Modern Industrial Society

All modern industrial societies lay legitimizing claim to democracy. Yet, even as certain democratic forms continue to exist, their content is more and more filled with the substance of administration and bureaucracy. As bureaucracy has grown, it has come to "rationalize" progressively more of human behavior, extending from (at first) production to other spheres of social life. In Theodore Lowi's words, its hallmark in the modern world has been *"rationality applied to social control."*[79] Phrased alternatively, this amounts to a contraction of the scope of citizenship in a modern industrial society and a concomitant expansion of the role of organizations as a medium between the individual and the larger society.

It is the nature of such organizations, and the manner in which they reconstitute the role of citizen, which are important here. Claus Offe has noted in this regard that this "institutional frame of reference . . . defines the citizen as the bearer of needs only within the sphere of which he is also a performing agent."[80] Citizenship, then, takes the form of what Lowi calls "corporatism" or "interest group liberalism."[81] Although it is certainly the case that the United States, having no interpenetrating or "focal" institution[82] such as the Communist Party, differs markedly from the Soviet Union in this respect, the upshot for the role of citizenship and the possibilities for democratic action which it contains seem quite analogous. That is, the individual *qua* citizen is *effectively* able to voice demands only through the organization(s) to which he belongs. The "rules of the game" specify that these demands must be negotiable; as Offe puts it, "they must offer concrete prospects for pragmatic success."[83] The consequences, as Offe sees them, are two-fold:

[First,] the formulation of negotiable bargaining positions can decidedly not take place within the association's internal forum. A bargaining strategy would deprive itself of all prospects for success if it were tied to the exhaustively debated directives and binding decisions of the membership. [Hence] internal democracy is lost.
[Second, this results in] a methodical and ongoing disciplining of members by the association's leaders, at least in organizations such as labor unions . . . which must deeply impress on their members the risks involved in "utopian" statements of their needs.[84]

In a word, individual citizenship becomes passive and defers to organization surrogates whose action is oriented toward incrementalism and support for the fundaments of the *status quo*.[85] Those who direct such organizations (whether industrial enterprises, labor unions, political parties or governmental agencies) are commonly called "administrators" or "administrative generalists."[86]

In the administered world of modern industrial society, citizenship yields to consumerism, just as political action gives way to "public opinion."[87] Man, in the bureaucratic world, Henry Jacoby reminds us:

is also expected to leave the matter of opposition to those competent to express it. When the authorities require an expression of opinon, they themselves ask for it. Such opinions are thus not instances of active social participation, but merely echoes of induced attitudes whose success is gauged by questionnaires.[88]

The contraction of citizenship in the modern industrial order has sharpened the tension between the normative basis of the political system, democracy, and the extant relations of bureaucratic power and government by administration. Within this tension we find a second major source of administrative ideology, a structurally rooted problem of modern industrialism to which a great part of this ideology is addressed.

3
Contradictions in Administrative Rationality

The penultimate step in unravelling the aspects of the ideology of administration brings to our consideration the core element in the administrative *Weltanschauung*, the concept of "rationality." We take this concept as it is articulated in the professional literature on administration, i.e., in the things which administrators read and write about themselves. Having so framed the concept, we begin in this chapter the final stage of our investigation, namely, locating at the level of thought the contradictions in administrative practice which find their symbolic resolution in ideology. Here we meet administrative ideology in its generality; by approaching it critically, we discover within it the source of "special ideologies of administration" which are offsprings of administrative thought refined to meet concrete conditions and to answer more specific questions encountered in practice. These special ideologies are discussed in Part Two. Our concern at this point is to examine their parentage.

The Immanent Rationality of Administration as a General Ideology

At the most general level, administrative ideology understands its object, administration, as a technical project emanating from technical needs. In both the Soviet and American professional literature on administration, we find explicitly or implicitly the following chain of reasoning and conclusions:

(1) There is underway in the world a process called the "scientific-technological revolution" which expresses the rationality of science. This process is a matter of fact which operates autonomously, i.e., it is not in any way socially or politically determined.

(2) This revolution has yielded a productive technology which is of great benefit to mankind.

(3) In order to fully exploit this technology, human organizations must reflect in themselves the same rationality which adheres in the scientific-technological revolution, and the technology which it has produced.[1]

The genesis of such organizations is commonly understood as a manifestation of human "cooperation," oriented toward the securing of "collective" purposes.[2] The rationality of science-technology expresses itself within these through the invention of organizational forms congruent with the given ("neutral") technology. Organizations structured in this way are, therefore, held to be the most "effective" and "efficient" means of utilizing the technology; in a word, the organization is itself "rational".[3]

Among American writers, Amatai Etzioni expresses this view very laconically. "Our society," he remarks, "is an organizational society . . . In contrast to earlier societies, modern society has placed a high moral value on rationality, effectiveness and efficiency . . . Modern civilization depends largely on organizations as the most rational and efficient form of social organization known . . . [serving] the needs of society and its citizens more efficiently than small and more natural human groupings such as families, friendship groups and communities."[4] Important here is the reification of "organization" and the attribution to it of human properties. Peter F. Drucker, for instance, believes that *"it is the organization rather than the individual which is productive in an industrial society."*[5] Similarly, Herbert A. Simon, defining the task of administrative "theory," claims that such a theory tries to locate *"the boundary between the rational and non-rational aspects of human social behavior."* It is "peculiarly the theory of bounded rationality—of the behavior of human beings who satisfice because they have not the wits to *maximize*."[6] It is the role of the administrator, then, to bring to fruition the rationality of the organization by attaining a congruence between its "logic" and the actual behavior of its members. This task can, of course, only be fulfilled when hierarchical relations (an arrangement of power which is often portrayed as "neutral"[7] or inevitable [8]) obtain. From his position atop the hierarchy, the administrator—viewing his subordinates as "human resources," as so much "stuff" to be manipulated via his control of rewards and punishments—undertakes to ensure that the "rationality" of the organization prevails over the "irrationality" of his members.[9] It is only the executive who commands a view of "the whole," it is only he who comprehends and, in a sense, embodies the "purpose" or "goal" or the organization; hence, it is only he who can direct the behavior of subordinates by manipulating the reward structure in such a way as to ensure their "compliance"[10] with the rationality of the organization which he, owing to his position, personifies.

The Soviets, for their part, have developed a view of administration and rationality which is in many ways remarkably similar to the American version just presented. Some of the "content," so to speak, is different (due, as we have noted, to contextual differences), yet the form—the appreciation of some sort of rationality which stands outside of or above men, divinable only by those initiated in the practice of administration—is identical. Herbert Marcuse has described this phenomenon as the "new rationality" of Soviet Marxism, two facets of which are of direct concern to us here:

(1) "The contradiction in Soviet society can be solved rationally, without 'explosion' on the basis of the socialist economy under the control and direction of the Soviet state."

(2) "The fundamental internal contradiction which provides the motor power for the transition to communism is that between the growing productive forces and the lagging relations of production. Its rational and controlled development makes for a gradual and administrative transition to communism."[11]

The first feature of Marcuse's conceptualization contains the kernel of what is manifest in Soviet ideology as a collection of "objective laws" which stand above the development of society and which, deciphered by the leadership in a quasi-mystical manner, provide guidance in policy making.[12] The second feature speaks directly to what we have called "technical rationality." In the Soviet case, there seems to be no sharp dividing line between the "objective laws" and the lower-level technical rationality, a situation due, I think, to the

Communist Party's claim to a monopoly on political leadership which is legitimated by doctrine (hence, all must be somehow doctrinally justified and the "objective laws" perform this function) and to the rather desultory collection of abstractions, projected hopes and apologetics which comprise the "objective laws" themselves. The reader of this Soviet literature never, to my knowledge, encounters of full codification of these laws,[13] nor is he informed of their derivation. All that is clear is that they somehow are thought to exist and that society, through the medium of the state, recognizes them and calculates its activities accordingly.[14] It is, for the Soviets, not the absence of objective laws, as Marx believed, but their recognition which distinguishes socialism from other epochs of human history.[15] Yet, from the standpoint of ideology, the importance of these "objective laws" cannot be overstated. Indeed, there has developed in the USSR an entire field of study, "scientific communism," which is defined as "*the science of the laws arising, established and developing in a communist order, of the paths and methods of the victory of the dictatorship of the proletariat, of the paths and means of constructing socialism and communism.*"[16]

Administration, in the Soviet view, is "scientific" inasmuch as it fits the behavior of people to the natural laws which have been discovered by "scientific communism." As S. S. Vishnevskii has stated it:

The major thing in scientific administration is the attaining of a correspondence of the subjective activities of people with the requirements of the objective laws.[17]

As successful administration in the USSR "depends on the knowledge and execution of the objective laws of socialism,"[18] so, conversely, "the administration of society on the basis of science goes forward in full measure as an inalienable feature of the natural law of socialist development."[19] In other words, one of the "objective laws" is that the "objective laws" are more and more recognized in the process of administration.

It may seem that administrative decision making is simply a question of applying this "scientific" understanding and bringing social relationships into consonance with the inevitable direction of history. We find, however, that the "objective laws" do not always operate automatically.[20] Sometimes, we might surmise, they need a little help from enlightened administrators.[21] For the most part, however, the Soviets believe that the "objective laws" tend to assert themselves, and administrators engaged in, say, social planning are depicted by Soviet writers as translating the content of these laws into the various concrete plans for society.[22]

Allowing for contextual difference, we can count the notion of "rationality" as the gravitational center of administrative ideology in both its American and Soviet versions. Rationality in its modern form, however, is not something peculiar to administrators themselves; it has taken root in societies organized along a bureaucratic pattern and is present within the very structure of knowledge and the gathering of information useful for administrative purposes;[23] *viz.*, the checking of social disequilibria through the extension of administrative "control."[24]

By exploring the dimensions of this concept further, we unfold a double-sided contradiction in "administrative rationality" from which spring administration's "special" ideologies.

The Dialectic of Efficiency and Effectiveness

Orthodox, administrative theorists, concerned much more with the problems encountered by bureaucrats than with the problem of bureaucracy *per se,* have developed the notion that rational organizations are those which embody the attributes of "efficiency and effectiveness"; it is the maximization of these qualities which, in their view, makes for "rationality."[25] In brief, "efficiency" is understood as a condition within the organization (a relationship between organizational outputs and the organizational costs of those outputs), while "effectiveness" implies a relationship between the organization and its environment upon which some "effect" is registered. At the root of this formulation lies the reified "organization," something which has supplanted men as the subjects of action and has rendered them as the objects of what might properly be called an alien force.[26] The concept of alienation is of central importance in demonstrating this. and in overturning the reification itself; an explanatory word, therefore, seems in order. Alienation is usually treated in orthodox administrative literature as a subjective phenomenon whose negative effects (poor motivation, absence of felt responsibility, etc.) should be overcome in the interest of more organizational efficiency and effectiveness.[27] This conceptualization ignores the objective side of alienation, an aspect of the concept which, when restored, reveals a fundamental contradiction in both bureaucratic practice and its reflection in bureaucratic ideology.

As a critical concept,[28] an understanding of human alienation begins with the conditions under which human beings reproduce themselves as social actors. Objectively, alienation then refers to the fact that within a bureaucratic situation, in which the labor of each is subdivided in detail, the material on which each works comes to him as "an other," as an "alien" thing (i.e., not his, from somewhere and someone else). Having performed his task upon such material, the individual then "alienates" it from himself (by, say, passing it along the assembly line to another worker, or through the object's eventual appropriation by the owner or manager of the enterprise). Consequently, we can say that the act of production involves a situation in which the individual is directed by alien forces (the production schedule, its content and pace), he has no control over the process and product of his labor, and that a key component of this process is the "self-alienation" of the individual—the incorporation of his labor into an object which is "not his" and which he alienates to another.[29] Combined with the objective side of this concept, i.e., a phenomenon imbedded in the structure of human relationships,[30] a subjective feeling of estrangement seems to grow and present for orthodox administrative thinkers the problem of "motivation" among subordinates.[31] As we mentioned above, the problem takes this subjective form because of the viewpoint of orthodox administrative theory. Given a reluctance to critically analyze the phenomenon of bureaucracy and preferring instead a "problem solving" approach to the difficulties faced by bureaucrats, orthodox writers tend to concentrate on methods for overcoming or mitigating the subjective consequences of alienation, rather than inquiring into its objective determinants.

Viewed dialectically, the mutually defining concepts of alienation and the subdivision of labor in detail are transmuted in orthodox administrative theory and take the form of efficiency and effectiveness, the hallmarks of organizational rationality. The following set of propositions outlines schematically the orthodox relationship between efficiency and effectiveness and examines why each, when developed, yields a contradiction requiring symbolic resolution in the form of "special" ideologies of administration.

A. Efficiency is dependent on effectiveness. Through the "rational" arrangement of operations within the organization (subdivision of labor) the rate at which individuals produce (alienate their labor) can be increased. The specialization of function which makes for organizational effectiveness simultaneously increases the internal efficiency of the organization.

B. Effectiveness is dependent on efficiency. The higher the level of internal efficiency, the greater the results ("effects") of organizational activity.

C_1. Efficiency is an individual property insofar as it is individuals who perform tasks.

C_2. Efficiency is an organizational property insofar as the results of efficiency (an improvement in the cost/benefit ratio) accrue to the organization.

C_3. Bureaucracy is a mediation between the performance of work and the product of that work. It transforms the individual (work) into the organizational (product).

C_4. As a mediation, bureaucracy inverts the terms mediated (1) in the sense described in C_3 and (2) by recasting individual efficiency in an organizational mold. The second inversion reveals administrative efficiency as a concept which contains (and for administrative ideology conceals)[32] a contradiction between the organization and the individual. The efficiency of the former increases at the expense of the efficiency of the latter.[33]

D. The same inverted relationships which hold for efficiency $(C_1 - C_4)$ are characteristic of effectiveness. The more labor is subdivided through specialization of functions, the greater (assuming such specialization is "rational") is the effectiveness of the organization. For the individual, however, the same process, by segmenting, simplifying and routinizing his task, renders him, *qua* individual, less effective.

The schema advanced above is simply one way of sorting out the contradiction locked up in "administrative rationality." Certainly, there are other ways to do the same. Reinhard Bendix, for instance, once discussed the problem of bureaucracy as that of a tension between the organizational demands on subordinates for compliance (to the formal authority structure) and initiative (required for performance and, equally, for improving performance[34].) Juxtaposing these conflicting demands to one another, it is not difficult to repeat the same exercise and, in so doing, to see organizations as internally contradictory task *cum* authority structures:

A. The authority structure of an organization depends, in the final analysis, on the organization's performance. Something must be performed or accomplished (even if only of a symbolic nature) in order to furnish the organization with the material means required to maintain compliance to its authority structure. There is no authority without performance.

B. There is no performance without authority. Performance under conditions of estrangement, conditions not only reflected in the structure of bureaucracy but *anticipated* by it,[35] is impossible unless it is in some measure elicited (and compelled) by authority.

C. The requirements of authority and performance are not congruent. Authority implies subordination to another (who bears responsibility) while performance implies initiative (responsibility on the part of the self) perhaps in violation of some established authority. More, authority is bounded in a bureaucratic organization; it has limits. Improved performance will encounter and attempt to push back such restrictions.

The point here is that once we have penetrated the reified facade of "the organization," the contradictions internal to its basic metabolism can be readily revealed in any number of ways. In exploring these contradictions we are simultaneously examining the bases of administration's "special ideologies."

Part Two
Special Ideologies of Administration

4
Ideologies of Administrative Leadership: The Mantle of Science

The Problem of Authority

Most accounts of administrative ideology have tended to base their analyses either on notions of "strains" in the administrative role or on the idea that ideology advances some administrative "interest." Under the so-called "strain theory," certain tensions or inconsistencies in the role of the administrator (say, uncertainty; or the problem of personal relations within the impersonal context of a competitive firm which may undercut such personal relations, and vica versa) call forth a "patterned response," an ideology, the "function" of which is to resta-bilize the administrative role.[1] The "interest" theory, on the other hand, sees ideology as the ideational stalking horse for some more or less tangible claim laid by administrators. Reinhard Bendix's work,[2] one of the best examples of this approach, examines how an interest in authority directs managerial ideology into exercises which legitimate administrative power as rightfully belonging to those of superior per-sonal qualities or, alternatively, as something naturalized in such a way as to occlude any question of its rightness.

There is much to learn from each of these approaches. Yet neither provides an exhaustive comprehension of its object, inasmuch as each depends on a "given" which it is at a loss to explain. Why, for instance, are there "strains" in the administrative role? Why do these strains, as Theodore Nichols[3] queries, yield *these* symbols, *this* ideology? Or, on the other side of the coin, why do administrators develop such a keen "interest" in advancing their own authority? Answers to questions such as these lie within the *structure* of modern industrial society and of the organizations which dominate its landscape, a structure which our argument so far suggests is permeated by the struggle among classes.

Within the formal framework of modern organizations this struggle plays itself out under differing conditions and exhibits a wide range of strategies, tactics and results. However, by pursuing further our line of inquiry, we can locate a common element in this struggle, a ubiquitous "source", so to speak, from which the strategies and tactics spring. Moreover, this formal organizational framework is structured, as we have seen, on the contrarieties of modern rationality. The *practice* of administration, guided by a contradictory principle, is *fundamentally* a contradictory practice. More specifically, the authority of the administrative superior, which is his by reason of formal position within the bureaucratic hierarchy, is sufficient to call forth compliance from subordinates. Yet, it does not of itself guarantee that the subordinates will take responsibility for their actions, that they will be "motivated" in the performance of the directives issued to them, that they will exercise initiative or ingenuity in their work. In order to attain preferred levels of performance from subordinates, to ensure that they display proper motivation and responsibility and so promote the *efficiency* of the organization, the administrator attempts to widen his sphere of influence over those below. In so doing, however, he goes beyond, and tends to subvert, the formal structure of rules and roles which establishes his position in the hierarchy.[4] This circumstance, a form of contradictory social practice which parallels the contradiction inherent in administrative rationality, is called, here, the "internal contradiction" of administration.

The concept of administration's internal contradiction sheds some light on the rather anomalous, yet oft observed,[5] behavior of subordinates within bureaucracies—their continued attempts at resuscitating the formal rules of the organization in order to enforce these *against* their superiors. Although it is these rules which, at bottom, place them in a position of subordination, those at the base of the hierarchy do have in formal stipulations a measure of defense against the arbitrary use of power by higher-ups. We need not reify these rules or exaggerate their durability in the face of administrative power (indeed, they often seem capable of remarkable change or rapid reinterpretation when used to challenge administrative power[6]—features of the rules which administrators include under the rubric, "flexibility"), in order to note their importance in the struggle internal to organizations. For the administrative superior, they confront him with a more or less permanent question: How to extend the scope of his control over subordinates "without undercutting his own authority?"[7]

James G. March and Herbert A. Simon, viewing this problem from the perspective of the administrator, put it thusly:

One problem in organizing control systems in complex organizations is to neutralize or eliminate the dysfunctional consequences of subgroup organization without destroying its ability to perform necessary functions. For example, organizations sometimes find difficulty in forcing lower-echelon leaders to conform to the demands of the hierarchy because some of the methods by which conformity can be most effectively enforced seriously undermine the leadership position of the supervisor.[8]

The problem of maintaining authority in the context of administrative practice which goes beyond the formal basis from which authority derives is answered by an administrative ideology of "leadership". In addition to highlighting the alleged moral and intellectual qualities of administrators, it provides them with a set of practical tools designed to extend the administrator's authority while leaving undisturbed the superior-subordinate relationship. The present chapter concerns itself with one face of the administrative Janus, leadership based upon a claim to "scientific" knowledge. The succeeding chapter deals with the second, "humane," face.

The "Scientific Management" of Frederick W. Taylor

In the United States, "scientific" administration dates from the work of Frederick W. Taylor. In *Principles of Scientific Management*,[9] Taylor explained how the worker could be turned into a more productive animal by structuring his motions in a manner analagous to those of a machine and by rewarding with higher pay the worker who out-performs his peers. The school of "scientific management" which Taylor founded seems particularly important to our concerns for a least four reasons. First, by fracturing each craft or skill into a number of simplified and routinized motions which require the coordination and supervision of non-productive employees, Taylor literally created the function of modern management. Second, in so doing, "scientific management" established a set of procedures or "laws" which exist outside the performing agents (men) and which govern the behavior of managers and workers alike. Third, Taylorism represented the initial attempt at a conscious, systematic structuring of human relationships around non-human processes and so set much of the tone for managerial thinking vis-a-vis human beings as things to be consciously manipulated, as human "resources." Finally, Taylorism employed the mystique of science to lend stature to a collection of rules-of-thumb designed simply, as Taylor often expressed it, to "get results."[10]

It would be difficult to exaggerate the impact of Taylor's work either with respect to contributing to the problem with which we are dealing, the internal contradiction, or with regard to presaging ways of surmounting or containing the effects (for management) of this problem in practice. The Taylor system introduced a "revolution," as Taylor was himself fond of saying, in the manner in which work was perceived, conceived and performed. Taylor was perhaps the first to understand that efficiency and effectiveness could only be carried to their logical conclusions by "collecting all slack from among employees," as Victor A. Thompson puts it. "The organization must try to reduce its costs or to shift them to employees and inmates."[11] Herein lies the significance of Taylor's attention to extrinsic reward. By simply denying that the worker has an interest in the content of his work *per se*, by claiming that monetary incentive is the rightful reason and reward for labor, Taylor could tackle the matter of work organization in a manner unfettered by any consideration other than organizational "efficiency" or, what is the same thing, "shifting the costs" to those who perform the work by progressively improving the ratio of organizational inputs to work(er) output.

In Taylor's hands, "science" meant that workers were things and may be treated accordingly. The consequences of such treatment with respect to the desideratum of "efficiency"—namely, what motivates the "things" to perform beyond the level of mere compliance—involved a problem which was not lost on Taylor himself. Firstly, he looked forward to the emergence of a "science" of "the motives which influence men,"[12] for knowing and manipulating these motives seemed a necessary precondition for overcoming the resistance to his innovations in organizational design. More, Taylor's "revolution" in conceptualizing organization and management can rightly be regarded as the forerunner of psychological testing and industrial psychology.[13] Taylor set for his approach the task of defining and knowing a job, a task accomplished by breaking up operations into their most elemental components and recombining these into "the one best way" (from the standpoint of organizational efficiency) of performing the operations. The other side of the equation, those who will man the segmented jobs so created, was an issue implicit in his method; indeed, references to "the right man for the job" were scattered throughout his work. Psychological testing and industrial psychology have attempted to locate "the right man" essentially be replicating Taylor's method in job design. That is, knowing the components of the job, these disciplines have searched for the "right man" to fill it. And the "right man" is known by application of a Tayloresque empiricism, adorned with "scientific" symbology, to the worker-thing, such that men appear simply as collections of measurable traits in quite the same way as jobs under the Taylor system are mere collections of measurable movements. The traits are "discovered" by observation and testing, matched to the job "requirements," and the circle of "scientific management" is complete.[14]

Finally, a minor theme in Taylor's work anticipated the ideology of "humane" administration which came into flower in the thirties. Taylor himself spoke of the manager's duty of showing "personal consideration for, and friendly contact with, his workmen which comes only from a genuine and kindly interest in the welfare of those under him."[15] Similarly, Taylor's followers addressed themselves to the "human" factor in industrial organization and saw as a part of their purpose:

To develop self-confidence and self-respect. . . self-expression and self-re-alization among the workers . . . . through the opportunity afforded for understanding one's own work specifically and of the plans and methods of work generally . . . [In a word] to build character through the proper conduct of work.[16]

Given the thrust of Taylor's teachings, one might question the place of such sentimentality in "science." This is the first of many occasions on which we shall meet cold-blooded calculation cohabi-tating with human warmth. This "odd couple", as Allyn Morrow and Frederick Thayer have called it,[17] is in no respect an odd coupling for administrative ideology, built as we have seen on contradictory principles and practices. Taylor's system was the first in a long series of ongoing efforts to surmount these contradictions in both thought and action. Like its successors which we consider below, Taylorism's core was a collection of empirical techniques structured around the "given" of organizational rationality. To this core was added scientific achievements or, better, natural science knowledge which had been converted into technological and engineering innovations. These innovations were in turn structured by the given or organizational rationality or, more prosaically, by profit, as David Noble has shown in his history of the engineering profession in the US.[18] The core itself, however, can be counted as "scientific" in only a nominal sense; only in the sense that ceaseless incantation of the word "science" plus the application of borrowed elements derived from the natural sciences (say, chemistry or metallurgy) is sufficient to summon credence, acceptance, and awe in the face of "scientific" management.[19]

The teachings of Taylor have enjoyed considerable success in the Soviet Union. In early 1918, Lenin put the matter thusly:

The Taylor system, the last word of capitalism in ["learning to work"], like all capitalist progress, is a combination of the subtle brutality of bourgeois exploitation and a number of its greatest scientific achievements in the field of analyzing mechanical motions during work, the elimination of superfluous and awkward motions, the working out of correct methods of work, the introduction of the best system of accounting and control, etc. The Soviet Republic must at all costs adopt all that is valuable in the achievements of science and technology in this field. The possibility of building socialism will be determined precisely by our success in combining the Soviet government and the Soviet organization of administration with the modern achievements of capitalism. We must organize in Russia the study and teaching of the Taylor system and systematically try it out and adapt it to our purposes.[20]

Lenin's admiration for all that was "scientific and progressive in the Taylor system" in particular, and capitalist management techniques in general, remains a feature of the current Soviet outlook.[21] To be sure, the Soviets eschew the "exploitative" nature of Taylorism and its latter-day descendants in capitalist countries, but they claim that since there is no exploitation in the USSR (by definition, it is "socialist") in these Western "scientific findings there are also valuable elements for us."[22]

In conformity with Taylorism's engineering bent, the Soviets feel that human organizations should be structured in accordance with the technology which is the infrastructure of economic and, by extension, social relationships.[23] Toward this end, a special academic discipline has emerged which is entitled the "scientific organization of labor" or, for short, *NOT (nauchnaya organizatsiya truda).* According to A.P. Volkov, *NOT* can be defined as:

the constant perfection on the basis of the development of technique of the scientifically based *division and coordination of labor.* It is the selection and introduction of the most rational and productive *types and methods of labor, the organization and servicing of the work place,* the securing of the best results and mutual linking of operations through utilizing rhythmic and evenly flowing work in the enterprise.

NOT is tantamount to a Soviet version of Taylor's "scientific management,"[25] and a number of its elements harken back to Taylor's method: an emphasis on organizing the work place so as to fulfill production tasks "with the smallest expenditure of muscular energy and nervous strain;"[26] the use of time study of the working day accomplished through "self-photographs;"[27] a recognition of how sociology and psychology can be used to boost labor productivity.[28] The Soviet context, however, requires some qualifications and emendations, as the titular difference—"scientific *management*" on the American side, scientific organization of *labor* on the Soviet— might suggest.

First, the absence of a labor market in the USSR, the relative dearth of competition for employment, means that "labor discipline," as we noted above, is a matter requiring conscious and constant attention in the Soviet Union. Lenin was the first to point this out, although his treatment of the subject was closer to sophistry than to critical analysis. Within a few weeks after the Bolshevik Revolution, Lenin was not only calling for organized mass competition in production, but was arguing that only in a socialist society does competition reach its zenith and give full throttle to the motor of industrial growth.[29] The Soviet stress on "socialist competition" might be seen as a surrogate for the discipline of the labor market, a discipline which the Taylor system tacitly presupposes. Labor discipline through "socialist competition" is articulated and consciously stimulated in the USSR as a fundamental element of *NOT.* "Socialist competition" is regarded as *"the basic form of raising the activity and initiative of the Soviet people,"*[30] as a "new and higher form of Soviet democracy,"[31] as educating the "New Soviet Man" and preparing thereby the advent of communism.[32] The juxtaposition of these contrary symbols—socialism and some of its characteristics (democracy, education) on the one hand, competition on the other—scarcely requires comment. As ideological statements, such pairings are to be expected. The same can be detected with respect to Soviet claims regarding the role of the working class in socialist competition and the manner in which "all the workers" press for the full implementation of *NOT.*[33] The working class is said to have something of a natural affinity to socialist competition, yet Soviet trade unions are enjoined to systematically stimulate it and to ensure that the working class comes to appreciate the merits of *NOT* in the event that some of the "objective laws," as it were, fail to operate automatically.[34]

Secondly, *NOT* tends to differ, at least by degree, from American "scientific management" (or "management science" as its latter day decendents are now called) inasmuch as it places a pronounced emphasis on a number of concerns and techniques not usually associated with its American counterpart. *NOT* seems a more multifarious combination of elements, perhaps because of the matter of political orthodoxy and state censorship which shapes the expression of administrative ideology in the Soviet Union. Unable to chart out separate schools or approaches, emphasizing one side or another of modern organizations ("human relations," "operations research," "organizational development," to name a few) with the same ease as their American cousins, Soviet ideologists tend to assemble a variegated panoply of ideas, symbols and techniques under the broad umbrella of *NOT.* One must understand *NOT,* according to V.D. Popkov, "not only as scientifically organized labor in a technical-organizational sense, but also as morally organized labor, based on relations of comradely cooperation and mutual assistance among the workers."[35] It involves "the creation of an atmosphere of *creative interest* in high results of labor, of a *good attitude* on the part of the workers."[36] Hand in hand with the *"furthest democratization of administration, by the broad attraction of all the workers to administration"* goes "the communist concern shown by workers for social production" and "the all-around development of the per-sonality."[37] Lest we forget, however, precisely who is in charge, to whom *NOT* belongs as a tool or organization, and what overall purpose it is designed to serve, consulting the same tracts yields:

It is primarily the administration and the specialists of the enterprise who bear responsibility for the components of labor organization.[38]

Expectedly, labor is to be organized to meet a specific purpose; viz., raise productivity and lower costs.[39] We find here a clue as to the concrete nature of "communism," a word with highpowered symbolic content as it appears in the eschatological passages of Soviet ideology. This comes in the explanation of the party's abiding concern with *NOT*.

The theses of the C.C. (Central Committee) of the CPSU conclusively show that the massive attention which the Party has given to the scientific organization of labor is conditioned not by the passing moment, but by the very character of the construction of communism, which is realized on the basis of science by the conscious forces of the entire people.[40]

In other words, communism in the flesh is the "scientific organi-zation of labor."[41]

In sum, Taylorism, originally an American phenomenon, seems equally at home in the USSR. Administration, say the Soviets, is common to all societies[42] and so "Lenin's assessment of Taylorism is of fundamental methodological importance; it would be naive to treat it merely as a characterization of one of the trends in the bourgeois theory of management."[43] Taylor's "scientific manage-ment" (as well as Henry Ford's assembly line) is presented by Soviet writers as precisely the sort of technique which, in conditions of socialism, contributes positively to the cause of human fulfillment by building communism.[44] In fact, one of the main strengths of socialism is said to be its ability to carry the "scientific-technological revolution" further and faster than is the case under capitalism.[45]

Systems Analysis

The word "systems" in postwar managerial thinking holds a status equivalent, from a symbolic point of view, to that occupied by "scientific" in the prewar period. Moreover, the practical implications of the "systems" approach—bringing "society under control in the same way as nature by reconstructing it according to the pattern of self-regulated systems of purposive-rational action and adaptive behavior"[46]—seem quite analogous to those of "scientific management," outlined above. So, too, does the methodological basis of systems analysis. Its proponents refer to it, in a manner reminiscent of Taylor's "mental revolution," as "primarily a way of thinking about the job of management,"[47] as a "frame of mind."[48] And like Taylorism, this "frame of mind" eschews the humanity of systems members, and substitutes in its stead a mechanical metaphor. People, reduced to "components," appear in systems thinking as objects. The subject, of course, is "the system."[49]

It seems likely that the work of administrative thinkers such as Luther Gulick[50] in the thirties set the stage for systems thinking in the postwar period, inasmuch as this work extended to the whole of an organization the rationalizing process which for Taylorism was effectively confined to the lower levels, the productive parts, of the bureaucratic hierarchy. Operations research, inaugurated during World War II, advanced this rationalizing process a long step by working out methods of integrating diverse sub-units around the task of solving complex technical problems.[51] Finally, cybernetics and computer technology lent respectively a sort of soul and body to the systems idea. The former contributed the notion of "steering" a complex system on the basis of information exchanges, the latter provided the technical means to accomplish this.[52]

As an administrative tool, systems analysis pivots on the question of bureaucracy's internal contradiction. That is, systems analysis in its basic design aims at arranging organizational substructures and processes in such a way as to obviate the need for command or direction, at least as those terms have been heretofore understood. Rather, the concept of "system" is defined as *"an array of components designed to accomplish a particular objective according to plan"*.[53] Reaching the objective involves systems controls—adjusting behavior when necessary to reach the "goal state"—which for the human "components" means manipulating the "key variables," viz., "motivation" on the part of subordinates, "leadership" for superiors.[54] The point, here, is that the "control center" exercises a sort of undetectable, and purely impersonal, form of control within the "systems" framework. It does not command, it "adjusts systems parameters."

In the layout of work operations, systems analysis does for the office what scientific management accomplished for the shop floor. It divorces conception from execution in such a way that what was "formerly the province of clerks" becomes "a factory operation."[55] In its more ambitious mood, the systems school aims at a peculiar transcendence of the conception/execution dichotomy through artificial intelligence, i.e., the writing of computer programs which enable the machines to do the thinking. The human "components" in such a universe suffer a corresponding demotion. As a systems proponent has put it:

As given future goals become increasingly clear, that is concretely defined, social behavior may increasingly resemble that of a servomechanism in which guidance is reduced to control . . . "by the margin of error at which the object stands at a given time [in Norbert Weiner's words] with reference to a relatively specific goal." Action may then become a routine problem of technical administration.[57]

In the Soviet Union, systems analysis and cybernetics initially met strong resistance from the guardians of the official ideology. By the late 1950's, however, these approaches were wholeheartedly adopted as scientific means of producing "communist abundance."[58] Presently, both are in vogue in the USSR, and Soviet writers go so far to stake the future of their country on the development and application of cybernetics to concerns extending from planning the national economy[59] to regulating individual behavior.[60] Noting the sharp technical-rational turn taken in Soviet thought, Peter C. Ludz feels that these Western approaches have been added to the Soviet arsenal of orthodox science in order to supplement an aged Marxism-Leninism no longer capable of generating solutions to the leadership's problems.[61] In Paul Cocks' assessment, qualified by both the author's restraint and the absence of any evidence, the turn to the systems approach has, in fact, contributed some solutions.[62] However, Stephen White is probably closer to the mark in noting that the conservative bias embedded in systems analysis appeals directly to a ruling group which is profoundly anti-revolutionary.[63] As if cognizant of the rub between revolutionary Marxism and technocratic systems analysis, Soviet authors indulge themselves in some rather ludicrous exercises in order to square this circle. The milder among these claims that:

The cybernetic approach to production does not contradict the Marxian view of social production as a system of social-productive relationships among people. On the contrary, under socialism it represents a more powerful means of conscious administration in correspondence with the tasks and goals established by society.[64]

Less restrained writers, however, purport that Marx himself was the pioneer of systems analysis.[65] Whether conscious of it or not, the "founders of dialectical materialism," say the Soviets, "elaborated . . . the general principles of the systems approach, and some of its specific methods . . . The Marxist approach to the study of society is a systems analysis."[66]

The systems approach in either society places a premium on information, the *conditio sine qua non* for administrative control of a given "system." Under its roof, then, systems analysis houses such sub-species as "social indicators" and "communications theory," each of which intends an objectification and quantification of systems' members (people) in order to maximize central administrative control. Again, the idea of control is indigenous to the concept of "information" as rendered in the systems scheme. Information is "that which can or does influence the comportment of another."[67] Social indicators on an aggregate scale,[68] and "communications," in a more individual vein, promise to entend the administrator's reach and include more of the human environment within his grasp. Reinhard Bendix, in his study of managerial ideologies, detected a certain character impressed upon "communication" by the bureaucratic mold; namely, "subordinates are expected to listen so they can learn, while managers merely receive information which they can use."[69] Hence, administrators portray "communications" as "simply a phase of employee relations,"[70] and since "obvious propaganda converts only the converted" they are advised to be skillful in "communications" in order to register the intended effect upon subordinates.[71]

The matter of control in the systems approach finds its most concrete expression and its quintessence in automation. From the subordinate's perspective, Andre Gorz's assessment is both pithy and perceptive. "After mechanization," he writes, "has dispossessed workers of all supervisory power and transferred it to separate agents, automation transfers the function of supervision to machines which now supervise their former supervisors."[72] Similarly, a study by J.R. Bright found that, in automated American industries, workers, having lost all control of the processes of production, additionally lose (as a group) most or all work-related skills.[73] When not replaced by machines, moreover, workers in some industries find that they have become interchangeable with them, as is true of General Motors new "PUMA" plan wherein robot and worker work side by side and substitute for one another on management's direction.[74] Automation, in a word, is impersonal control completely carried through.[75]

From the point of view of the administrative superior, however, things look otherwise. Incredibly, automation is said to restore to the worker "a sense of function in an industrial environment that is socially integrated," giving him a new and enlarged feeling of "responsibility."[76] In quite the same manner, Soviet writers assert that "automation establishes labor as creative;" from a pure act of execution it is transformed into "an act of self-directed quest, the setting and solving of tasks, of spiritual enrichment and self-actualizing of the individual (leading to) the all-around and harmonious development of the human personality, the education of the individual, the unification in him of spiritual wealth, moral purity and physical perfection."[77] Again, the Soviets claim the speedy introduction of automation as one of the chief advantages of "socialism,"[78] and echo the technocratic claim that automation raises, rather than lowers, "the general level of education and technical training of the workers."[79] Under communism, we hear, automation will have abolished physical labor,[80] on the one hand, and the division of labor (and, consequently, class distinctions) on the other.[81] American writers are, however, slightly less sanguine. "Fifteen years from now [1969]", opines Warren Bennis, "40 percent of the work force will have positions in problem-solving organizations . . . 40 percent will be social change agents . . . 20 percent will do the remaining unprogrammed, low-level jobs of the society—cab drivers, sweepers, kitchen help."[82] Apparently, a sort of "four-fifths" communism is on the American agenda for 1984.[83]

An Assessment

The totalitarian implications of systems analysis, a society of preprogrammed people processors,[84] is tempered by considerable evidence that systems analysis, when measured against its grandiose self-advertisements, has been a resounding flop. Ida R. Hoos,[85] for instance, has convincingly demonstrated that the use of systems analysis in American government has amounted to a mystifying and expensive shell-game played by a cast who, combining the characteristics of high-priests and con-artists, have created a language (intelligible only to insiders) which trivializes the problems which they set for themselves, essentially by reducing all social phenomena to questions of engineering. Peering up from its procrustean bed, the patient, society, is assured by the engineer/physician either that his problems have been "solved," or that a solution is imminent, awaiting only a few technical adjustments. In short, the practical value of systems analysis for Hoos, and for others such as Robert Lilienfeld,[86] has been its semantic infusion into bureaucratic ideology of pretentious, "scientific " jargon.

It would be a mistake, I think, simply to dismiss the operational utility of systems analysis. But equally mistaken would be an evaluation of its worth which did not situate it within its social context. As we have seen, systems advocates appear quite keen to dismiss out of hand certain features of modern industrialism which render it problematic, conflict-ridden and unstable, features such as the enormous concentration of power in large organizations, the degradation of work and alienation. Yet it is precisely such features which provide systems analysis with its *raison d'etre* and *modus operandi.*

Systems analysis and its armory of computer hardware purport to make decision-making an optimalized, scientific process. Yet Graham Bannock, in his study of major American corporations, discovered in case after case that the scientific paraphernalia was no more than *post facto* legitimation for decisions already reached by top executives. When the computer printout did not conform to the executive consensus it was the print-out and not the consensus which found its way to the dust bin.[87] Similarly, I.L. Horowitz and J.E. Katz, in their survey of the role of social scientists in influencing public policy in the US, discovered that power, not knowledge, was the key factor. Social science may legitimate elite consensus, but as a challenge to such, social science is all but impotent.[88] And so for various organizational techniques which claim "scientific" status. The personal element can be severed from personnel decisions, for example, by means of a testing medium which determines the "right man" for the job. The fact that the test "instrument" has no effective, much less "scientific," basis does not occlude the salutory result which such a procedure has in buttressing organizational power. Those denied placement or promotion, on the one hand, are hardly in a position to question "scientific" decisions; those who receive employment or who are promoted, on the other, receive as well the impression that their talents have been "scientifically" validated. As a consequence, they tend to exhibit increased motivation in the pursuit of organizational objectives.[89]

"Scientific administration" succeeds on bureaucracy's tacit terms. It does not measure up to the claims made for it by administration's ideologues, but that is beside the point. Its success is better guaged by viewing it in the context of social and organizational power, by seeing its source point in bureaucracy's internal contradiction. From this perspective we find in the systems style of organizational design a method for enlarging the scope of control exercised by the top over those below. More, the systems approach changes qualitatively the nature of the control itself, replacing, in its advanced forms, human direction by machine monitoring. Systems analysis alters, then, the contours of the organization's "contested terrain" in favor of administrative power. It, likewise, as the scion to the "scientific" tradition in administrative ideology, contributes an image of administrative power which naturalizes such power, at least in its immediate appearances. Within the ambit of this ideology there is no room for discretion, personal considerations or human judgment. All is reduced to a facticity which deflects any challenge to its operation or its effects as uninformed, purely emotional or "unscientific". Finally, this image is of no small import in legitimating administrative leadership by grounding it in the unshakeable surety of science. On this foundation are built the castles of administrative "humanism."

5
Ideologies of Administrative Leadership: "Humane" Administration

Within the borders of bureaucratic ideology reside a number of images of administrative "leadership." One of these, leadership based on a supposed "scientific" knowledge, we met in the previous chapter. Here we encounter others: leadership which accrues to the administrator by virtue of his inherent qualities and talents; leadership which is grounded in the moral altrusim of the administrative superior; leadership which is bestowed on the administrator by appreciative subordinates; leadership which the administrator shares with subordinates via their participation in decision making. These images are not always harmonious in their substantive implications. For instance, the cold-blooded leadership qualities associated with the "scientific" side of administrative ideology do not neatly mesh with the warm-hearted personability advocated by the human relations school. Consequently, in accounting for these apparent inconsistencies, we would do well to bear in mind the contradictory basis of bureaucracy from which the images spring. Our focus, then, is on the manner in which these images ideologically surmount bureaucracy's internal contradiction by supplementing the *formal* authority of the administrator with a *personal* claim to "leadership." And such a personal claim is not registered in the abstract. It is integrally connected to the tools which the ideology provides for effecting the posture and practice of administrative leadership.

61

Images of Leadership

In the United States, the long tradition of the "administrative gener-alist," a tradition which dates back at least to Taylor's "scientific man-agement,"[1] is synonymous with the development of the special status and role contained in the term "administrative leadership." In the Soviet Union, the official doctrine of a "workers' state" had tended to militate against the staking out of a particular and privileged niche for professional administrators.[2] By the 1960's, however, Soviet manage-rial training, as documented by Barry M. Richman,[3] had come to reflect a growing concern with the preparation of generalists. In the 1970's, this tendency reached fruition with the establishment of a new curricu-lum at the Moscow Engineering/Economics Institute leading to the degree of "specialist in information." As one factory director remarked on the occasion of this new professional orientation, "the specialist in administration *must not be trained for a definite branch* [of production] *since the basic principles of administration are everywhere the same.*"[4] A new institution, the USSR Academy of the National Economy, was estab-lished in October of 1978 for the specific purpose of training a new cadre of administrative generalists. Its director, D.M. Gvishiani, has characterized the current Soviet approach to managerial training as having:

successfully overcome the narrow technical approach to the industrial enter-prise, which should be regarded as a socio-economic organism, a complex entity of diverse relations. Sociological investigations of the process of man-agement are gradually reaching beyond the mere description of managerial activity and seek to discover the laws and new forms and methods of management corresponding to the historical tasks of creating the material and technical basis of communism, with all possible speed. The theory of management, which sprang from the need to ensure maximum effectiveness of co-functioning systems, is surging ahead and becoming an independent branch of science.[5]

The fact that the top political leadership in the USSR has lent its voice to the chorus praising professional administrators as the lead-ing element in society[6]—in the face, of course, of the official doctri-nal heritage of a "workers' state"—should indicate how much head-way the ideology of administration has made in the Soviet Union.

In the United States, a definitive statement on administrative leadership was put forward in 1929 by H. S. Person, then Managing Director of the Taylor Society. Person's characterization has subsequently been developed and embellished by other writers, but the major ideas which he advanced have remained the core of American thinking on this matter. "Leadership", he wrote:

> is not passive; it is an active composite ability to induce [not impose] understanding, conviction, desire and action *in a manner which leaves no disturbing impression on the mechanics of the induction.* Every executive is a leader of a sort, but successfully to achieve a development of scientific management in an enterprise he must be that type known as a creative leader; one under whose leadership [quoting Ordway Tead] "the purposes and objects will find most ready reception at the hands of those led which can most readily be seen by them to square with their own desires which they can quite readily and naturally take up as their own." The more creative the leadership at the top, the more creative, although of course not uniformly so, will leadership become all along the line.[7]

These thoughts concisely express both the problem inherent in the administrative role and the ideology's solution to it. How can the administrator overcome the limitations of his formal authority in order to secure better performance below? Simply, he becomes a "creative leader," "creative" in such a way as to surreptitiously induce in subordinates a feeling that the goals of the organization, *his* goals, are actually *their* goals.

In accomplishing this feat, the administrator influences his subordinates by his "ability . . . to manipulate the appropriate rewards,"[8] be they material or symbolic. With particular attention to the latter, the "creative" leader seeks to convert his organization into an institution, meaning, *"to infuse with value* beyond the technical requirements of the task at hand."[9] As part of this value infusion administrators are advised to manufacture ideologies for their respective organizations[10] which hopefully provide a focus of symbolic identification for subordinates[11] and a moral code for them to follow. As Chester A. Barnard puts it:

> The distinguishing mark of the executive responsibility is that it requires not merely conformance to a complex code of morals but also the creation of a moral code for others . . . that will result in subordinating individual interest and the minor dictates of personal codes to the good of the cooperative whole.[12]

The ideology of administration recognizes and articulates the relational nature of leadership. The "creative leader" personifies such. His *leadership* is the type which elicits *motivation* from subordinates. The ideology, however, does not shy away from ascribing to the administrative leader personally a number of innate qualities. The administrative leader is one of superior knowledge,[13] a "philosopher"[14] who upholds "high ethical standards."[15] His persona has a sort of charisma about it, and is enveloped by a corona of personal loyalty emanating from subordinates.[16] He is a man having "such courage and acting upon it [that] over time this becomes transformed into a kind of corporate courage that permeates the entire organization."[17] The administrative leader is an understanding individual who has "a sensitivity to the needs and motivations of others,"[18] which enables him to "cultivate" his underlings, and grow around him a garden of similarly creative, self-actualizing people.[19] As we shall see, the notion of "self-actualization," as rendered by administrative ideology, translates as redoubled effort to secure organizational objectives. In the context of "leadership," we might note the ideology's emphasis on the administrator's alleged ability to improve organizational performance by radiating an energy which subordinates reflect. "To be genuinely motivated," writes Michael G. Blansfield:

all men must have a real sense of contribution; *this must start at the very top and spread downward*. Without the motivation that a sense of contribution provides, employees cannot have the strong drive to improve themselves and their performance. Here, then, lies the challenge to the top management.[20]

From the Soviet quarter, we find a repetition of the same themes. *Rukovodstvo* (administrative leadership), for instance, is defined in a manner quite comparable to Person's conception.

Rukovodstvo emerges as the personal management by the individual who directs a productive subdivision or unit of administration, and includes . . . the making of decisions and their execution. It follows to *distinguish personal leadership from administration as a whole*. Administration includes all functions (planning, coordinating) *rukovodstvo* is one of the functions of administration *on which depends for the most part the success of administration*. It is incorrect to consider the concept of *rukovodstvo* within the framework of administration, as was done in the early era of the development of scientific administration. In contemporary conditions, *the stimulation and direction of the activities of subordinates emerges as the main thing* in the realization of that function.[21]

Quite like his American counterpart, the Soviet *rukovoditel'* is said to possess innately a number of sterling personal qualities,[22] which extend from the mundane to the eschatological: "organizing ability, precision and punctuality, a proper bearing, charm, the ability to get along with people,"[23] a high "moral consciousness [and] a deep understanding of the interests of the workers."[24] So equipped, the *rukovoditel'* stands "as an example, as a model in everything which concerns the execution of his duty before the state and its laws,"[25] both at work and in life.[26] He is:

a person of political vision, tempered by ideas, deeply knowing all sides of the affairs in his charge, able to create the incentives [which yield] the most effective, highest quality work and responsibility for its execution. He is a principled person, able to subordinate his own interests to the interests of the collective . . . a modest and simple person in dealings with other people, regardless of their station in the enterprise, showing unceasing concern for people and their welfare.[27]

Since administration is "in the main the *administration of people,*"[28] the *rukovoditel'*is one who builds for himself an edifice of "personal authority" in his relations with subordinates.[29] Indeed, "the single property without which successful administration is impossible is the conquest of *authority by the leader.*"[30] The *rukovoditel'*,in this respect, must "be able to inspire with enthusiasm and captivate his subordinates,"[31] while at the same time developing among them "a creative approach to their work" which generates a "feeling of self-esteem."[32] Of prime importance in this endeavor is the administrator's ability to structure relations with subordinates in such a way as to inculcate in them an identification with the organization and its goals,[33] promoting, thereby, more initiative and creativity on their part.[34]

This brand of Soviet "self-actualization" for subordinates is not advocated for its own sake. Increased production, the improvement of organizational performance by means of generating more responsibility below, is the purpose served.[35] And, toward that end, the Soviets mobilize all manner of unlikely candidates, as if to compensate for the absence of the labor maket's impersonal discipline. One example is the electoral campaign at election time. In addition to recounting the achievements of the regime, the campaing is designed to promote more enthusiasm at work and is regarded by the authorities as a means of fulfilling the economic plan.[36] Another example would be those elected to public office, the deputies of the soviets. Deputies are portrayed as "from us, with us and like us," yet, they are said to be a cut above the norm both in terms of their morality and performance at work.[37] And the function of the "people's representatives" is primarily production oriented. That is, in their places of employment, deputies are to set the example and the pace for improved organizational performance.[38]

The goal of improving organizational performance likewise guides the approach taken by the administrator toward those in his charge. The posture which he strikes—"comradely," "authoritarian," "passive"—depends upon that which produces the best results in a given situation.[39] In each country, however, the preferred form, *ceteris paribus,* appears to be the "comradely" or "participative" style, the tools for effecting which are part of the ideology's more practical side.

Tools of Leadership

"Human Relations"

The advent of "human relations" can be properly dated from the celebrated Hawthorne experiments, conducted by a team of Harvard industrial psychologists led by Elton Mayo, who founded the new school. In brief, the findings at Hawthorne led to the inference that interpersonal relations in the work setting, the so-called "social world of work," was the key variable influencing the rate of production. Consequently, management's approach to subordinates was in future conditioned by two general considerations: (1) the work group, not the individual, is the unit of production and, hence, the proper focus of managerial concerns;[40] (2) improvements in production can be best brought about by "a freer and more pleasant working environment, a supervisor who is not regarded as a 'boss' [and, therefore] a 'higher morale' [among employees]."[41] On the one hand, then, human relations, by emphasizing the emotional state of the worker, tended to count symbolic rewards for workers as more influential than material ones in attaining managerial goals. On the other, the securing of managerial objectives was henceforth seen as contingent upon the ability of the superior to induce his respective work group to adopt as its own the goals and norms which management prescribed.

The emphasis on symbolic incentives should not be mistaken for a reversal of scientific management's orientation toward extrinsic rewards. The supervisor's appreciative hand on one's back is no more an *intrinsic* gratification for work than is the pay envelope. Human relations does not address the question of job design. It merely takes task structures and authority relationships as situational givens and goes on to make some sweeping and, it might be said, rather silly claims regarding the possibility of an intrinsically fulfilling work life within the modern organization, even for "elevator operators, janitors and manual laborers."[42] If we can say with Hedy Brown that degraded work in modern organizations "relays to the individual the low opinion society or a particular management extends to him,"[43] then human relations can be seen as an effort to overcome the force and consequences of this perception on the part of workers, to "disguise," in J. Carpentier's words, "the graver consequences of excessive division of work."[44]

Human relations attempts to displace the effects of the internal contradiction in managerial practice by removing labor/management conflict[45] and substituting in its place "cooperation."[46] The strategy designed to bring about this transubstantiation depends upon human relations specialists who are, of course, hired by those in authority, but who in order to win the workers' confidence comport themselves in such a way as not to be perceived by workers as part of the authority structure.[47] Through both counselling and casual conversation, the human relationists acquire access to the world of the workers' subculture. They identify the informal leaders, the norms and the institutions (patterned resistance to administrative authority) of work groups and convey this information back to their employers.[48]

For human relationists, such practices are considered to be a genuine service to workers, inasmuch as the only road to "personal development" is one paved by an active acceptance of management's goals.[49] This one-dimensional view of organizations is embedded in the methodology of human relations. Beginning with the proposition that the organization is rational and that top management personifies this rationality, resistance to administrative authority can only be "irrational." Since workers offer resistance, it is up to human relations to "prepare the emotional worker for the more rational decision making process" by encouraging him to "accept responsibility for his feelings."[50] For human relationists, workers seem quite incapable of either rational thought or cognitive statement. When workers articulate administrative infringements on their basic human dignity or grievances at being denied the necessities of life, human relationists interpret such remarks as "felt injustices."[51] The trick, it would seem, is to reduce the worker to an entity which "feels" (not thinks) and then to channel his emotional energy toward organizational goals by converting the feelings into "positive motivation."[52]

The practical side of human relations ideology brings an extension of administrative control into the processes internal to informal work groups and the life of the individual outside work. Its symbolic side denies that such is in any way a manipulative practice. Rather, the ideology holds that it is an effort to "educate, guide and direct their [workers'] activities toward a pleasant and effective result," making, thereby, "Human Relations--The New Frontier."[53] Equally, the attention which the ideology gives to the "human factor" is supplemented by the supposed "scientific analysis" which human relations brings to bear on its subject matter.[54]

In the hands of capitalists, say the Soviets, human relations is a tool of exploitation, deceit and manipulation.[55] However, quite like Taylorism, this same tool in "socialist" hands is regarded as a powerful implement for humanizing work relationships and propelling society toward communism. Soviet administrative literature is marked by the same preoccupation which American writers, influenced by the human relations approach, evince with respect to the "human factor,"[56] in general, and the "work group,"[57] in particular. E.E. Vendrov and L.I. Umanskii, for example, stress the importance for the *rukovoditel'*of inquiring into the dynamics of the work group, the goals of its individual members, their backgrounds and leisure time activities in the interest of exploiting these factors as resources for management's objectives.[58] Similarly, B.D. Lebin and M.N. Perfil'ev speak of the necessity of a knowledge of "human relations" ("*chelovecheskikh otnoshenii*") on the part of administrators, claiming that:

The effectiveness . . . of the cadres of the apparatus of administration depends in large part on the degree to which they are acquainted with the basic motives of human behavior and psychology, on the ability to listen to people, and to learn their opinion and to respond to them.[59]

The point is to shape the personal interests and goals of the worker, through the correct application of "material and moral incentives," to fit those of the organization, the state and the Party.[60] And toward this end, the collective should be harnessed as a means of social pressure "in order to bring the individual in line with the larger unit."[61]

Two aspects of human relations merit a word before we consider some of its more sophisticated offspring. First, Mayo's experiments at Hawthorne, which supposedly provided the "scientific" basis for the human relations approach, in fact generated data which in no way support the conclusions reached by the human relationists.[62] Hence, it may be that a hidden agenda was smuggled in and out of the Western Electric plant where the experiments were conducted, an agenda tailored perhaps to the taste of the industrial psychologists. For the ideology of human relations transforms management's mercenaries into healers ministering to workers wounded needlessly by the bureaucratic regimen. As we shall see later in this chapter, the "human" element tends to bulk larger for those who counsel administrators than it does for administrators themselves.

Second, human relations seems only of marginal significance in advancing its practical goal, increasing organizational performance.[63] For an approach which understands its object, workers, as brainless beings, this comes as no surprise. Workers know well enough the nature of the factory system and their resistance to it can hardly be expected to be broken by such administrative charades. What emerges, then, is the ideological element, the refurbishing of managerial images and a set of tools, however crude, for grappling with bureaucracy's internal contradiction. Administrative receptivity to human relations might be understood from this perspective. For instance, a survey of 114 American business firms carried out by the Bureau of National Affairs in 1959 found that 90 per cent of the executives in the sample believed that human relations had a more important effect on productivity than did material incentives, "although some of them pointed out that it is difficult to supply proof of this belief."[64] Although human relations has not succeeded in producing happy workers, the same need not be said with regard to administrators.

Advanced Human Relations

If scientific management viewed the worker as essentially a pair of hands and human relations saw in him a heart, the species of administrative ideology to which we now turn directs its interest to the worker's head. Aside from the many fine words which the ideology employs—"human growth," "self-actualization," "employee participation"—the purpose of the tools here considered is straightforward enough. By extending the scope of its conception to include more of the individual, more of the individual's energy can be enlisted in the pursuit of organizational objectives.

The work of Abraham Maslow is of seminal importance for what I am calling "advanced human relations." His ideas on personality and motivation have exercised a powerful influence on most of the American writers of this genre. Maslow developed a view of human nature which locates the motivation for activity in a sequence of unfolding needs, arranged in a "hierarchy." At the base of this "hierarchy" are physiological requirements (food, shelter and so on), after which follow more or less emotional needs (safety, belongingness), and finally, at the apex, the need for "self-actualization," or becoming all one is capable of becoming. Maslow believed that once a need was satisfied, it no longer acted as a motivator. Additional motivation could only come from the next rung on the needs' ladder.[65] The message for administrators was clear: material incentives (scientific management) have satisfied workers' physiological needs; emotional happiness (human relations) has taken care of the needs for recognition and belonging; motivation in the present and future depends on the ability of workers to satisfy their needs to be whole, "self-actualizing" individuals. Management, on Maslow's instruction, is then an exercise in arranging organizational circumstances such that the "higher" needs can be met. For there is no essential difference, said Maslow, between the organizational and the individual "good." "Healthy" organizations are populated by "healthy" individuals striving for individual/organizational goals.[66]

As attractive as Maslow's ideas have become for many American administrators and writers on administration, there are a number of reasons to doubt their soundness. As William Leiss has shown, Maslow's efforts to unlock the secrets of human nature are sundered from any cultural context. It may be that in modern industrial society (where life is fragmented into work and leisure, home and employment, private self and public self) such a "hierarchy of needs" has a certain plausibility. But to apply this notion to man across cultures and throughout history, as Maslow does, is not only unwarranted and ethnocentric, it is simply wrong.[67] To this conceptual difficulty might be added the fact that a "hierarchy of needs" has not been supported in empirical investigations.[68] Finally, as David Schuman argues, Maslow's ideas pertain to administrative style, they do not engage the question of bureaucracy as a system of power.[69] As such, the appealing array of symbols in Maslow's work might best be understood as just that, appealing symbols. They conceal a substantive interest of quite another order, namely, developing "hard drivers" *totally* committed to *selflessly* striving for organizational goals from which, paradoxically (or ideologically), the "hard drivers" derive their *own* needs-satisfaction.

As Maslow was working out the bases of "eupsychian management," another administrative writer, Peter F. Drucker, was developing a parallel line of thought oriented more closely to managerial practice. It seems to me that the fusion of these two strands, the grandiloquent (Maslow's) and the strategic (Drucker's), in administrative ideology has produced the particular compound of "advanced human relations."

Drucker put forward the idea that an untapped source of productivity resides in the attitude (cognitive and emotive) of the worker. By tapping this source, by promoting a "managerial attitude" among all members of an organization, regardless of their respective ranks, the primary desideratum (*"higher productivity and profitability, that is . . . better economic performance"*) could be attained.[70] The practice of management, Drucker believed, implies:

consideration of the human being as a resource—that is, as something having peculiar physiological properties, abilities and limitations as the properties of any other resource, e.g., copper. It implies also the consideration of the human resource as human beings, having . . . personality, citizenship, control over whether they work, how much and how well, and thus requiring motivation, participation, satisfaction, incentives and rewards, leadership, status and function. And it is management, and management alone, that can satisfy these requirements.[71]

Drucker's method of "management by objectives"[72] was conceived as a vehicle for "satisfying these requirements" in such a way as to boost productivity and profits.

Human beings, Drucker believed, perform best at those tasks in which they have invested something of themselves; they work most diligently in attaining those goals which are their own.[73] The concept of management by objectives, then, means that:

every manager should responsibly participate in the development of the objectives of the higher unit of which he is a part.[74]

Beyond this, management must evoke from workers a "positive motivation" by allowing for the worker's participation in the coordination of his task with that of others (although the goal-setting function of the enterprise remains the prerogative of management).[75] In so doing, management by objectives:

substitutes for control from the outside the stricter more exacting and more effective control from the inside. It motivates the manager to action not because somebody tells him to do something or talks him into doing it, but because the objective needs of the task demand it . . . [and] . . . he himself decides that he has to—he acts, in other words, as a free man . . . it insures performance by converting objective needs into personal goals. And this is genuine freedom, freedom under the law.[76]

In, apparently, equal measure:

The enterprise must expect of the worker not the passive acceptance of a physical chore, but the active assumption of responsibility for the enterprise's results.[77]

A disciple of Maslow, Douglas McGregor, has extended Drucker's thinking on these matters. McGregor believed that the way in which management treats employees determines the "nature," so to speak, of the employees themselves. Under what he called "Theory X" management, superiors regard their underlings as inherently lazy, motivated only by material reward and in need of close supervision and constant direction. "Theory Y" management, on the other hand, reverses this perspective. It views the worker as keen to take responsibility for his job, to invest his energy in goals which he himself identifies, to extend (in both senses of the word) his self in the organization.[78] Consequently, McGregor believed that "the essential task of management is to arrange organizational conditions and methods of operation so that people can achieve their own goals *best* by directing their *own* efforts toward organizational objectives."[79] To this species of "participation" he assigned the term "democratic management." Yet he was quick to point out that democratic management:

does not mean abdication [by management]; it does not imply that "everyone decides everything." Its essence is that it makes effective use of human resources through participation; it provides general rather than close supervision; it is "employee centered"; it encourages responsible behavior and tough-minded self-control [on the part of subordinates] rather than reliance on external authority.[80]

He also saw additional payoffs for management in the scheme, for:

When resistance to or sabotage of managerial decisions is anticipated, participation provides a natural method for minimizing or eliminating them [resistance and sabotage] in advance.[81]

As with Drucker, productive results are the key value to be obtained through "democratic management."[82]

McGregor, however, explicitly addressed the question of human freedom in the context of behavioral control and, in so doing, seems to have established the rudiments of a conventional credo which underscores the more "advanced " approaches to administration in both the public and privates spheres. While it is difficult to treat McGregor's thinking on this subject as anything other than a melange of sophistries, it is perhaps important to outline his argument as representative of certain ideological orientations endemic to administrative thought. In brief, McGregor asserted that behavioral control constitutes the opposite of "constraint," and, since freedom is also the opposite of constraint, behavioral control actually enlarges freedom. In this respect:

the removal of constraint involves the manipulation of a variety of system variables . . . not the elimination of control . . . [and] . . . in this case these actions give human beings more freedom, not less![83]

Acknowledging the "risk" involved in such an endeavor, McGregor cast the problem of stepped-up productivity through applied social science in transcendental tones. "Shall we limit ourselves" he asked, "to primitive methods for helping mankind solve the problems that beset us, because we fear the responsibility for choice that knowledge brings?"[84]

In consonance with the general perspective of the "human factor," a number of related approaches and specific techniques have emerged which promise to increase organizational performance through "self-actualizing," "motivated" and "participating" employees. Despite a plethora of labels—"action research,"[85] "group dynamics,"[86] "organizational development"[87]—which advertise their respective cures for what ails modern organizations and their members, these approaches share a common method and metaphor. Namely, "change" is brought about by means of a "change agent's" intervention in the organization. This "change agent" (employed, of course, by top management) "diagnoses" the organization's problems and prescribes (to top management) any number of remedies. Medically-derived language is quite common in this field, and medically-derived practices, such as "sensitivity training" and "encounter groups" are principal instruments for administering therapy, for creating "healthy" organizations. In this context, "health," as might be expected, is yet another word for productivity. And, here, appearances seem to count for everything; "attitudes," "perceptions," "feelings" are the targets of these techniques, the things which are to be changed. As one proponent states the case:

As a result of these positive feelings, there often tends to be less bureaucracy in the organization and a feeling of freedom by the individual to do his job. The employee tries to do his job well, not because "they" make him, but because he wants to.[89]

The symbol of "science" seems to have been found by organizational humanitarians as serviceable as any other. The credo claims that "behavioral science" is at last "a legitimate science with its own technology."[90] For administration, it is much more of a "legitimating

science," the technology of which is designed to increase managerial control.[91] In its own vernacular, applied social "science" is
"change oriented" and management, skilled in social science techniques, can itself act as a "change agent" improving the lives of
employees both on and off the job.[92] (Indeed, some claim that
behavioral science techniques can be employed to "change" personnel practices in such a way as to yield a "new type of administrator,"
one who is creative, inventive and otherwise admirably equipped to
deal with change itself.)[93] Yet, we might ask: What sort of changes
does applied behavioralism promise the administrator? And, here,
the answer is direct enough; change which will eliminate "the cause
of social illness" and promote "aggressive progress through systematic development."[94] This, in short, is the incantation of the social
engineer who sees his satan in the form of "outmoded culture" and
believes that through the correct application of behavioral science
hocus pocus he can exorcise the demon, "human conflict."[95]

This ideology sustains a compelling image of a hero-administra-
tor, armed with scientific knowledge, sallying forth to slay any
number of modern dragons. Yet these images intermesh with contrasting hyperbole addressed to the task of "humanizing" organizations by hiding their internal hierachies. Here, the administrator is
counselled to juggle the formal rules of his respective bureaucracy in
such a way as to tap more deeply the organization's "human resources."[96] Participatory management seems the most popular
scheme for extending to subordinates the invitation to disbelieve in
bureaucracy, to pretend to a psuedo-equality which will provide a
suitable setting for eliciting more of their energies.

Empirical evidence from case studies and laboratory experiments
indicates that, within the context of a hierarchical organization, the
participation of subordinates in decision making actually *decreases*
their relative power vis-a-vis superiors.[97] As the term, "participation," appears in administrative ideology, however, it inverts this
empirical relationship. By taking on the contextual richness of related symbols, "participation" becomes the avenue to "self-actualization," personal "growth," "health" and so forth. It is in this
respect that "participation" becomes a material force. On the one
hand, it contributes indirectly to overcoming bureaucracy's internal
contradiction by legitimating directives from the top with the aura of
an alleged involvement of those below. The directive is not im-

posed, rather, it is put forward as the product of a "democratic" decision-making process. On the other hand, it intends directly to reverse the consequences of the internal contradiction. Its proponents argue that, properly approached, the participation of subordinates can effectively expand administrative control over the work group, especially by using the group's informal leader(s) as a bridge from management to workers.[98] Participatory management, then, "can be viewed as a device permitting management to participate more fully in the making of decisions,"[99] and in securing greater motivation from subordinates in carrying out the decisions themselves. Hence, experiments are said to reveal that when a "group as a whole make a decision to have its members change their behavior, [it] was from two to ten times as effective in producing actual changes as was a lecture presenting exhortation to change."[100] Similarly, survey-questionnaire techniques are put forward as a means of obtaining desired information from subordinates, with the bonus that the morale of subordinates seems to improve by the very fact that such a survey (implying that someone is interested in what they think) occurs.[101] In short, "participatory management" is a euphemism for "managed participation." As proponents note, "if the [participatory] gathering is not managed effectively, the result can be wasteful and perhaps even destructive."[102]

Interestingly, many Soviet writers on administration have appropriated not only the perspective and techniques found in the American literature, but employ as well the same terminology and labels. V. Maslov, for example, describes something called "heuristic" management, a term which was coined by the American writer, William F. Gore. In either instance, the meaning of the "heuristic" approach is quite the same; namely, it aims at suffusing the formal organization with a layer of the irrational or emotional, inasmuch as this, it is believed, will channel the potentially disruptive emotions of individual members toward organizational goals and tap, thereby, new reservoirs of energy and creativity.[103] Attitude surveys, conducted among subordinates, are equally appreciated by Soviet writers as tools of motivation, as well as new sources of information for administrators.[104] Like their American counterparts, *rukovoditeli* are instructed to show an interest in their subordinates in the belief that the symbolic benefits thereby bestowed will constitute a more powerful source of motivation than mere material incentives.[105] Similarly, administrative leaders are expected to "understand the motives of others,"[106] and to engage in personal counselling which involves both the subordinates' on-the-job activity and his leisure time pursuits.[107] Through such personal contact, the "needs" of subordinates can be, purportedly, adjusted to those of administration, such that the former is in no way compelled (he acts out of his own "unconscious habits") in fulfilling directives from above.[108]

The Soviets are also cognizant of the work group, "the collective," as the pivot of organizational performance. Consequently, Soviet writers lay great stress on the ability of the *rukovoditel'* to motivate the individual through the proper structuring of group norms and goals.[109] Always the goals of the group should be made to reflect those of the larger organization, meaning that "the worker evaluates his own actions in light of the politics of the CPSU and the Soviet government."[110] Having internalized the organization's goals as his own, the worker enjoys maximum "freedom and autonomy," which, however, "does not exclude but presupposes the control and examination of his actions" by superiors.[111] As such, the *rukovoditel'* takes "an active part in the formulation" of the views of subordinates and does so with tact, "not offending another person's convictions, but only promoting change in their convictions in what is necessary for the leader of the administration."[112]

Participatory management bulks large in Soviet administrative ideology. The *rukovoditel'* is counselled to actively involve others in the decisions which he has taken.[113] As Omarova has stated it:

The major consideration here is to nurture in the workers a feeling of direct participation not only toward what is being done in the work place, in the enterprise, but in all the branches of the national economy. Each worker must be convinced that his opinion is received with all [due] attention, that he has of necessity not a formal, but a full and real right of a voice in the decision of the most important questions of administration. . . .

Obviously, an order will remain on paper if it is not enlightened by people, creating around it a common opinion and a corresponding frame of mind.[114]

Along with the interest shown by *rukovoditeli* toward their subordinates and the opportunity for the latter to "feel" that they participate in the decisions of the former, work becomes "the foremost of life's needs,"[115] a "creative act,"[116] a "source of joy and pleasure."[117] In this respect, the Soviets pay no small attention to the application of social science—"a lever for the regulation of social relations . . . a force serving progress"[118]—to the problems of the administrator. Programmatically, Volkov has stated it thusly:

> In the conditions of the transition of society from socialism to communism, the problems of the individual, his physical and spiritual capabilities, is one of the central *sociological problems of the scientific organization of labor*, the solution of which is a necessary condition of the transformation of labor into the primary necessity of life.[119]

In future, we are told, *rukovoditeli* will look upon their organizations as "social-psychological laboratories," and with an education spanning philosophy, psychology and sociology, they will be prepared for "comprehending the moving motives of people and collectives as a whole, [knowing] the specific needs of their subordinates and also the relative force of their various desires."[120] Consequently, social science is hailed as a force directly serving "communist construction."[121] In addition to applying the techniques of industrial psychology to subordinates, Soviet writers, in the manner of their American counterparts, assert that social sciences can package programs for selecting "creative" superiors. As L. A. Sergienko and A. S. Kokovin have remarked:

> Selection according to a set questionnaire does not in many cases guarantee [that the right people will be selected], and therefore the importance of other methods of solving this question is growing. One such method, in particular, is the utilization of special tests for admission to the state service. These tests are able not only to highlight the psychological features of the individual personality, but also his fitness for the concrete duty of the work in the sense of possessing organizational talents, being able to make well-reasoned decisions and similar things, and to clearly disclose the executive character of the worker's capabilities.[122]

In all, the application of social science to administrative matters serves in the Soviet Union, no less than in the United States, as a link between the mundane matter of increasing production and the eschatological pronouncements on "self-actualizing" and "socially conscious" subordinates and superiors. It is presented as a tool for such; its users, regardless of how blunt the instrument may be, can count it as a weapon in the legitimation of administrative power; we can number it among the elements of an ideology springing from the contradiction discussed in this chapter.

Some Empirical Findings

The responses to bureaucracy's internal contradiction, reviewed in this chapter and in the preceding one, represent reconstructions of administrative ideology from its most fully-articulated variant, the professional literature on administration. What can be said about this ideology, however, as it appears in the group consciousness of administrators themselves? In order (1) to provide an answer to this question, (2) to empirically ground the concept of administrative ideology and (3) to qualify the concept's relevance to those who practice administration as opposed to those who study, write about and teach it, a series of interviews was conducted in each country with local government officials and with those who provide professional training to them. The interviews employed the open-ended or non-directed technique. The purpose of this approach is, of course, to elicit as much direct or "pure" information as possible from the respondent—"pure," inasmuch as the respondent is not given concrete questions containing ideas which may be foreign to his own way of looking at things. Rather, general questions or topical themes are supplied. These the respondent can interpret in his own fashion and comment upon as he sees fit.

Because of the nature of the research undertaken, and the places in which it was carried out, it was unfortunately impossible to ask the same open-ended questions to all respondents in the sample. This shortcoming is, I think, more a matter of form than of content. In each case the purpose of the interview format was to encourage the respondent to discuss his work and his relations with others in that regard. Since the various open-ended questions which were used appeared to succeed on that score, their variation across the sub-sets in the sample does not, as far as I can determine, represent a serious flaw in the method. These sub-sets are:

(1) Thirty-five interviews with city officials (city managers, city councilmen, department heads, city clerks, and so forth) which were conducted in 1973-74 in a midwestern state. These respondents were all asked the following questions:

  (a) What do you like about your work?

(b) What do you dislike about your work?

(c) What would you like to see changed/improved in this respect?

(2) Eight interviews in a western state with directors, faculty and, in
one case, an administrative officer, of six post-graduate public
administration programs. These were carried out in 1977. The
questions asked of these were:

(a) What are the best features of your program?

(b) What shortcomings or problems do you see in your program?

(c) What would you like to see changed/improved?

(3) Interviews with thirteen local officials in three large cities in the
European part of the USSR during 1979. Numbered among
these were secretaries of the executive committees of city, re-
gional (*oblast'*) and district (*raion*) soviets, the heads of major
departments of the executive committees of city and *raion* soviets and a vice chairman of the executive committee of a *raion*
soviet. The respective questions asked were:

(a) With respect to bringing the citizens into the process of
government, what in your district (region, city) is being
carried out particularly well?

(b) On the same topic, what insufficiencies or shortcomings do
you notice?

(c) What would you recommend as improvements for the future?

(4) Five interviews with directors or faculty of five university programs or special institutes engaged in providing pre-entry or
post-entry professional training to local officials or technical
assistance to local government in the USSR. All of these respondents reside in one city, but many travel extensively throughout
European Russia (and, in one case, Siberia) as part of their work.
These interviews were also conducted in 1979, and the questions used were the same as those asked of sub-set (3) with the
difference, of course, that these respondents were giving their
views as knowledgeable observors, teachers and trainers rather
than as participants in the matter under consideration.

The duration of these interviews ran from 30-45 minutes with the
first group, approximately one hour for those in the second group,
from one hour to two and a half hours with group three and one to two
hours with the fourth group.

In comparing the administrative ideology as reconstructed from the professional literature with the data obtained through interviews with the four sub-sets in the sample, three overarching generalizations are immediately possible:

(a) The most highly articulated, coherent and unqualified form taken by this ideology is to be found in the respective professional literature on administration in these two countries.

(b) The construct is also well-grounded empirically among those who teach, train and study administrators (hereafter referred to as "academics").

(c) Those actually engaged in the practice of administration (hereafter, "practitioners") speak with at least two voices. On the one hand, they are given to discussing abstract or general questions in a manner which conforms to the ideal type construct. On the other, they continually depart from, and often contradict, the precepts of the ideal type when discussing immediate and/or concrete matters.

Rather than summarize the data in tables or with statistics, I have chosen a format which presents particular comments made by individual respondents. These comments were selected inasmuch as they typify themes raised by a number of respondents during the interviews.

Soviet Practitioners and Academics. The manner in which ideology is shaped by practice, or one's relative distance from practice, was evident at every turn during the course of these interviews. Soviet academics, although often critical of the working operations of local government, were much more inclined to present an idealized picture of local government and administration than were practitioners. Whereas academics would ordinarily begin their responses with a discourse on the present stage of "communist construction," the growing political activity of the citizenry, the further democratization of social and political life, and so forth, practitioners would usually commence with a recitation of aggregate statistics on such matters as how many cubic meters of housing space have been constructed during the current five-year plan, how many meters of asphalt laid, and the like. It struck me that the significance of each prologue was probably commensurate in communicative value. That is, each was a means of constituting the speaker before the interviewer rather than a transfer of information *per se.* Each contained a marked ideological element. However, the difference in content, eschatological on the one hand, mundane on the other, underscored the relative differences obtaining between academics and practitioners. Interestingly, soviet deputies who did not hold an administrative position did not volunteer long (and, it can be said, rather empty) recitations of statistics, although in most cases these deputies clearly knew a great deal about the work of their respective soviets. To name the difference between academics and practitioners regarding their respective orientations we might use the terms "ideology of results" in reference to the latter and "ideology of signification" with respect to the former.[123] We shall have recourse to these names in what follows.

Consistent with this first distinction is the tendency exhibited by many practitioners to emphasize results or performance at the expense of signification. For example, academics were unanimous in calling attention to the moral and educational aspects of serving in social organizations. Those who, without pay, patrol the streets *(druzhina)*, who attend to order (physical and political) in the neighborhood (house committees or street committees), who sit in judgment over their peers for petty offenses (comrades' courts) are, according to academics, democratizing social and political life, acquiring an education in "the school of administration," preparing the advent of full communism. Practitioners, although mentioning such things in passing, would underline the assistance they receive from these organizations. "We are unable, it is unthinkable," as one put it, "to work without the help of the *druzhina*." Equally, the desideratum of more facile control over the performance of subordinates led some practitioners into an effective advocation of both a labor and services market. The incongruence of this advocacy with respect to the official ideology would scarcely require comment. We might note, however, the juxtaposition of academics to practitioners on this matter of "results" versus "signification."

The question of training also evinces a difference in the outlook and attitudes of the respective groups. All spoke of a need to continue to improve the work of local government. Often, training was cited as the central feature of such improvements. Yet, when academics spoke of training, they tended to use the language of signification. For example:

I would rather see "naive" students graduating from this institution than ones who know the ways of the world and "how to get things done." Such people, being "naive," are likely to uphold the law, are likely to try to do what is right rather than what is merely expedient. They will learn the ways of the world soon enough anyway.

Practitioners, on the other hand, tended to view training through the prism of pragmatism.

> It often happens that an individual summoned before a comrades' court has no respect for this institution and not the slightest intention of obeying the ruling of the court. What does the chairman of the court do? He usually makes matters worse by pounding his gavel and demanding respect. By becoming angry. This is why we must train such people in the proper approach.

Similarly, academics tended to emphasize that the training and technical assistance provided to deputies of local soviets "raised their activity" from the point of view of deputies as representatives of the population. Knowledgeable representatives, it would seem, have at least the potential for being effective representatives. Although practitioners would use the same phrase, "raising the activity of the deputies" with at least equal frequency, they seemed to have a separate notion of activity—executing decisions rather than making them. As one put it: "The most important part of the education which we provide to deputies is familiarizing them with recent Party directives."

Finally, the issue of information and its use within organizations tended to divide the groups. Although often critical of the amount of information made available by local soviets regarding their own work, academics would point out that more information, more reporting by administrative bodies and legislative commissions, is available today than has been heretofore true. This has made it possible to know more about the operations of government, to criticize and hold responsible those who fall short of their obligations to the citizenry. Practitioners also count this increase in information as a significant advance. They often tend to see it in slightly different terms, however. On the one hand, more information from more sources assists them in controlling their own subordinates. As for the critical aspect of information, this is largely regarded as ritual as my question to a top-level administrator makes clear.

> *Question:* Why is it that of all the units performing this operation in the city, these units in these districts were singled out by the city soviet for criticism? What is wrong in those districts, why are they performing so poorly?
> *Answer:* [With a broad smile] That is simple. They are not performing

poorly, it was just their turn to be criticized. Next year, it will be someone else's turn.

American Practitioners and Academics. By way of contrast, the first thing which might be mentioned is that the American academics in the sample seemed a much more divergent group than did their Soviet counterparts. One group, those employed in programs of a very practical bent, tended to eschew what they called "ivory towerism" and instead emphasized training students to be successful administrators in the so-called "real world." A second group seemed much more reflective. As one remarked:

We bring students to the understanding that reality, especially administrative reality, is really someone's invention, someone's definition of what is and what isn't. We try to get the students to ask: "Whose invention?" "Why was it invented *in this way?*" "For whose purpose?" "What could be different?"

Although this second group was by far the smaller of the two, its existence nonetheless distinguishes the American academics from the relatively more homogenous Soviet sub-set. It might be said that the ideology of signification was more weakly represented among some in the American sample, as the following remark by an academic would suggest: "We don't see a lot of reading [in the curriculum] as all that important. Besides, what's in the textbooks is largely irrelevant to real life."

It may be that systemic difference are at play here. In the United States, a capitalist country, popular ideology seldom takes the form of dogma. Usually it exhibits the more subtle, closer-to-life features of a market economy wherein "fair exchange" tends to depoliticize ideological thought. Consequently, explicit justifications for social reality are not as important as they are in a Soviet-type system which, lacking such a depoliticizing institution, seems to require a greater degree of explicit signification in order to legitimate what exists.

Irrespective of this marked divergence in the outlook of American academics regarding the level of signification employed, there was an equally marked tendency for them to assume that either the training or the educational agenda should not be set by the trainee or the student. With respect to full-time courses of academic study, the following comments (the first from a subject who exhibited a relatively high level of signification, the second from one whose level of such was much lower) are relatively representative of the entire sample on this count:

Almost all students who come into this program really have no idea of either how to approach the subject of administration or what they can actually accomplish in the way of promoting change once they become administrators.

We don't expect the students to make the synthesis of theory and application; it must be made by the teacher in class.

And, for in-service training, the same seems to hold:

He [the local official] knows he's hurting and he knows what feels good, but he's unable to make a judgment on what type of training he needs.

What the local people [officials] want is not what they need.

We have to identify [their] primary needs such as goal-setting and interpersonal relations.

The "we know best" attitude among academics vis-a-vis practitioners is also present among administrators vis-a-vis their subordinates. Here, two features of the intra-organizational situation seem to stand out. First, more could be done by subordinates, but for some unspecified reason, it is not.

Trying to motivate our men could be a full-time job.

In city government, people should sell themselves, just like in business.

We need to improve the psychological space of employees. There's not enough initiative.

Some academics paid considerable attention to "organizational humanism," suggesting that a key function of the administrative superior is to actively engage subordinates in decision making within the organization. Practitioners, however, were inclined to mention this much less frequently. "Motivation," it appeared, stopped short of "participation." When this topic was addressed, however, its substance seemed to subvert its symbology:

We should do more to involve the employee in the affairs of his department. Employees, through such participation, will develop a positive self-image, they'll perform if they feel more a part of things . . . (pause) . . . In other words, [we] con 'em.

Concluding Observations

It may be that a peculiar feature of modern administration, the specialization of work according to a subdivision of labor, penetrates the ideology of administration as well. That is, as the interview data would indicate, the ideology is itself subdivided into an eschatological version, more common to academics, and a variant associated with practitioners which stresses practical results. This subdivision does not seem to be a rigid one. The differences between academics and practitioners are more often matters of degree than qualitative distinctions. However, the differences do appear marked enough to invite some speculation.

With respect to the "human relations" approach to management, we noted the emergence of a new administrative imperative—workers must be treated as (at least "feeling") human beings—which was not actually derived from the experimental data on which it was purportedly based. If "humane" administration is largely the invention of academics, and our interview data would suggest this too, then we might tentatively conclude that this side of the ideology appears the more pronounced the further the remove from administrative practice. For practitioners, it may be something of a background ideology. It establishes a general climate, it can be drawn upon when issues or problems related to it come to the fore, it provides some tools which may be of practical use. But apparently it is neither valued for its own sake nor prominent in the everyday outlook of practitioners.

The images of leadership reviewed in this chapter also indicate certain inconsistencies in the ideology. Overcoming the internal contradiction in administrative practice seems in both the American and Soviet cases to involve the conversion of the administrator's *formal* authority into a *personal* authority. Hence, the ideology emphasizes the superior qualities of the administrator and his talent, knowledge, sensitivity to and concern for subordinates. Yet the tools which the ideology provides for effecting this leadership, principally, "participatory management," would seem to blur the very authority relationships which personal leadership strives to promote. The reason so far advanced to account for contradictions of this type is the contradictory basis of administrative practice from which the ideology is generated. The implication of these contradictions in administrative ideology, however, is a topic to which we return after taking up bureaucracy's external contradiction and ideologies related thereto.

6
Ideologies of Democratic Bureaucracy In the United States

Strictly speaking, the title of this chapter contains a contradiction in terms. Namely, the words "democracy" and "bureaucracy," as concepts referring to the structure and distribution of power in human action, are antipodal. Bureaucracy signifies a set of relationships in which power is drained, so to speak, from the performing members of an organization and lodged at the apex of the organization's hierarchy. Top administration enacts rules and procedures which control the behavior of performing members in such a way as to reproduce its own power on an expanded scale. Channeling more human energy toward the pursuit of organizational objectives is, in such a context, merely another way of saying that the reservoir of power at the disposal of the command structure has been increased. Democracy, on the other hand, is predicated upon the reverse of this situation; power, in this case, is distributed across all points in the structure and the action of each member derives either from self-direction or from group norms or rules which reflect in their content the self-direction of the members who have collectively established them.

In modern industrial society, we have noted that bureaucratic forms of organization predominate, and that, for the two societies under consideration, this situation stands in opposition to the formal set of public norms which are rooted in the democratic tradition. Consequently, we can speak of an "external contradiction" as that obtaining between the democratic norms (themselves, emptied of meaning over time, taking on the status of myth) of these two societies and the actual policy-making practice of administrators. In symbolically surmounting this contradiction, administrative ideology leans heavily on the images of "leadership" which we outlined in the two preceding chapters. In brief, this aspect of the ideology asserts that administrators do and should make decisions for society because: (1) they are the only ones equipped with sufficient expertise and (2) they have highly developed social consciences (as well as other outstanding moral qualities) and, therefore, wield power so as to secure the interests of "the people." In addition, a second aspect of the ideologies deriving from the external contradiction effects a conceptual revision of the normative context in which the practice of administration occurs. Here, we find two apparently conflicting tendencies. One asks that traditional democratic values, now rendered obsolete by the increasing complexity of modern industrial society, surrender to the claims of "realism." The other portends the fulfillment of democracy's promise through sounder, more enlightened administration.

This chapter outlines the American version of administrative ideology's response to the external contradiction. Inasmuch as Soviet historical traditions and their related symbologies differ markedly from the American, they are treated separately in the following chapter. However, the three tendencies apparent in administrative ideology with respect to overcoming the external contradiction are directly comparable in either case. These tendencies are: (1) a redefinition of democratic norms, (2) the ascription of democratic leadership to those occupying administrative positions and (3) recasting bureaucracy as a "representative" institution.

Redefining the Normative Context

Prior to World War II, Dwight Waldo[1] documented the emergence of an ideology of administrative rule in the United States which portrayed administrators as a new "guardian class."[2] This ideology has continued to grow unabatedly. As Waldo noticed, the traditional, American concept of democracy has been revised by this ideology so as to harmonize it with the presence of such "guardians." Democracy, he pointed out, has been twisted into the shape of "better management."[3]

In the administrative state there is scarce room for citizens. Decisions of public import are said to be too "complex" to be deliberated upon and decided by the public itself. Administrative experts are required for this. The corresponding demotion of the population from active subjects to passive objects is indicated as well in the naming of the administrative state's inhabitants: "citizens" have been replaced by "consumers." Christopher Lasch[4] and David Dickson[5] are no doubt correct in calling attention to the parallel here between Taylorism and the eclipse of citizenship in the US. Taylorism made for "efficient" administration by removing the control of production from workers and vesting it in management. "Effective" government in the modern state likewise looks to administrative specialists for policy direction. Active citizenship is perceived as something which undermines this "effectiveness." The Trilateral Commission's report, *The Crisis of Democracy*, represents one of the more extreme versions of this view. Without more political apathy on the part of Americans, the report contends, the political system will become "overloaded." American democracy in this respect is already a "threat to itself." The nature of this threat is said to derive from democratic incursions into the structure of socioeconomic inequality in the US, incursions which somehow destroy "cooperation among citizens" and "create obstacles to collaboration for any common purpose."[6]

A more straightforward argument which the ideology of administration directs against democracy derives more from a notion of managerial pragmatism than from the undesirability of democracy *per se*. The contention from this quarter is that the United States "is swiftly moving from Jacksonian democracy to a democracy which is simply more workable in the modern climate."[7] According to John Kemeny, chairman of the presidential commission which investigated the nuclear accident at Three Mile Island, this movement has been completed. "Jacksonian democracy," he believes, "cannot work in the year 1980—the world has become too complex."[8] The "more workable" democracy required in the modern world seems an idea which is interchangeable with increasing the power of right-minded administrators, a project which, some hold,[9] will produce an improved democracy. This variant sees modern administration in both the public and private sectors as "expanding the frontiers of human development and initiative."[10] Less sanguine spokesmen, arguing that the need for "competence" has made Jacksonian democracy impossible,[11] caution administrators to maintain the myth of democracy and to supplement it with their own moral qualities. As Eugene P. Drovin and Robert H. Simmons counsel:

Democratic government . . . has little meaning except within the context of certain transcendent values. Executive power exercised within the framework of the theory of democratic processes and institutions cannot, therefore, claim legitimacy except within the bounds of fundamental values which are compatible with democratic theory. The public service and the public interest are fused; one makes little sense without the other.[12]

So fused, democratic "myths serve to sustain confidence that government operates the way it should, [for] to be aware of the inner workings of the political process might make government intolerable."[13] For the initiated, however, "we recognize that ours is an administrative *culture* and, so recognizing, take action to improve and extend this culture."[14] Indeed, those who do not appreciate this alleged fact have been diagnosed as suffering from "bureausis," a disease to which "ultra-conservatives" seem most prone.[15]

Administrators and Democratic Leadership

The ideology of administration sees administrators as a "governing class."[16] As a 1970 task force on social goals reported to the American Society for Public Administration:

Administrators find themselves having to make more and more policy in league with each other, and having to draft most of the legislation that is theoretically handed to them as a mandate. . . .
Public executives, taken as a group, have not yet awakened to the fact that they are in charge. They are responsible for the operation of our society; they cannot wait around for somebody to tell them what to do. If they don't know the answers, we're lost.[17]

Government by administration bases its legitimacy in part on the peculiar properties attributed to administrators. First, the professional literature abounds with claims to the effect that administrators, and they alone, possess the "competence" or "expertise" required to govern effectively. These qualities translate roughly as "professionalism." In order to establish the posture and bearing suited to shouldering the public burden, the administrator is advised to polish his professional image, something which "gives us [academics and practitioners] more purchase than any other orienting idea."[18] This aspect of the ideology can be traced to the cult of expertise and neutral competence, so much in vogue during the

Progressive era and further propagated by the school of "scientific management."

In the same way that Frederick Taylor and his disciples created the institution of modern industrial management, the Progressive reformers invented professional political administrators, albeit, under the guise of eliminating "politics" from government.[19] The model according to which the reformers sought to perfect a government free of politics was the modern business corporation. Considering the class base of the reform movement, this is hardly surprising.[20] Reform propagandists were given to describing governments as "vast businesses" whose "stockholders" are the respective citizens,[21] and whose elected officials comprise "small boards of directors."[22] Sound business practice was portrayed as more or less synonymous with political democracy. In the case of municipal reform and the Commission Plan which first instituted Progressive hopes in city government, reformers believed that:

There is one thing about making improvements under the commission form of government. It is possible to transact business. . . . The new form of government is the instrument with which business can be transacted. It pleases the people. It gives the people more and more direct power.[23]

For the Council-Manager Plan (which, as more closely tailored to business specifications, tended to supplant the commission plan), reformers explained that:

Happily, the idea of a business corporation is largely synonymous with efficiency, in the minds of the American people. The design of running a city in the same excellent way was received with profound satisfaction.[24]

The pinnacle of the Progressive pantheon in municipal government was occupied, of course, by the city manager. He was typically portrayed as an "expert" directing other "experts" toward "good government," and fulfilling the "deep conviction" of the American people in the business system, harkening to their "demand" for more business in government.[25]

This idea of "more business, less politics" in urban administration was from the onset equivalent to placing business interests at the top of the governmental agenda. The nature of the reforms militated against the participation of working people in local politics,[26] while

the symbol of "professionalism" spearheaded the ideological struggle against democracy. This symbol seems today no less a powerful
legitimation for administrators when confronted by democratic resistance to their power. For instance, in summing up the recent
history of the public referendum in Texas as a method for granting
the right to city employees to organize in trade unions, I. B. Helburn
and D. T. Barnum remark that:

Although public management can sometimes benefit from a situation
where the cry of higher taxes or loss of citizen control automatically brings
out a large conservative vote, this is a two edged sword. If the socioeconomic character of the electorate favors primarily with the workers, for
example, then city management may be forced to adopt resolutions that
professionals would never have made. Based on the Texas experience,
therefore, we feel that issues involving complex personnel and labor relations decisions should be made by professionals.[27]

In addition to the mystique of "professionalism," "expertise" and
so forth, a second symbolic strand is woven into the ideology of
administrative leadership, a strand which emphasizes the "morality" which administrators are said to bring to the job of governing.
As such, administrators are depicted as embodying, within their
own outlook, "the public interest."[28] Dvorin and Simmons put it this
way:

The most highly educated, technically competent, and civically aware
segment of society must become active in the delineation of the general
public interest. Bureaucracy has probably grown too powerful under modern conditions to be controlled wholly by external institutions acting as
obstacles. It is essential that control come from within the bureaucracy
itself. The essential condition, however, is a set of values extending far
beyond bureaucracy's traditional concerns.[29]

Somewhat ironically, a notion of atonement appears explicitly as
one of the elements in the new credo.[30] That is, public administration is seen as culpable for any number of contemporary problems;
hence, the emphasis is on setting things aright by means of enlightened administrators acting with a social conscience.[31] The argument
is most explicitly stated by the "New Public Administration" group
and runs essentially as follows:

Administrators are not neutral. They should be committed to both good management and social equity as values, things to be achieved or rationales . . . [N]ew Public Administration seeks to change those policies and structures that systematically inhibit social equity.[32]

Administration, it would appear, should be a social vehicle whose destination is the good life.[33] And the more autonomous its operation, the more "freedom" at the disposal of administrators, the more "responsibly" it is likely to perform in the cause of social justice. As McGregor saw behavioral control contributing to the freedom of those controlled, so "the essential congruence of administrative freedom and political freedom must be recognized."[34]

Representative Administration and Democratic Bureaucracy

These considerations of moral rectitude and social conscience on the part of administrators overlap to some extent with the third tendency in America administrative ideology under discussion, here, i.e., the notion that bureaucracy is, or can be made to be, "democratic" or "representative." Milder forms of this claim purport that administration is democratic insofar as administrators act in the "interests of all the people."[35] These interests are, however, not necessarily articulated by all, or for that matter, any of "the people." Enlightened administrators, blessed with the gift of "intuition,"[36] are alleged to be capable of divining these interests themselves. As a city manager has commented:

We have the best interests of our cities at heart. That is our job, and that is what we work for. We must broaden our concept of managerial duties and *not wait for the council or even the citizens to propose actions* which we believe the council should consider.[37]

Of course, it is preferred that the city manager "sensitize" the council to the extant problems and needs[38] (we shall come to this tactic shortly), so that he acts in conjunction with formally representative bodies. Nonetheless, "by taking a general view of the city's needs and coordinating its many-sided development effort, he [the manager] is a guardian of interests not ordinarily represented on the council."[39]

An important part of the "guardian" posture of administrators is their self-styled image of "change agent." The "change agent" mystique calls on the administrator to act as a "catalyst in need articulation and problem definition."[40] Equipped with a vision of social justice and skilled in "interpersonal relations,"[41] the administrator is expected to use the leverage of his position to see to it that public policy reflects the needs of the disadvantaged.

Particularly in the area of municipal government, we find a steady evolution in this direction. In the prewar era, city managers were held to be apolitical administrators whose task it was to implement the policies of elected city officials. Although expected to assist in the formulation of such policies, the city manager's base of legitimacy was precisely this apolitical or neutral stance.[42] Studies of the council-manager form of government supported the neutral-professional characterization, either because politics was conceived solely as an electoral process,[43] or because "educating" the public with respect to the merits of a particular program was not construed as a political activity.[44]

After World War II, revised thinking about public administration and its political aspects made its impact at the municipal level. City managers began debating among themselves the extent of their policy-making role and the ethics of such.[45] In 1952, the Code of Ethics of the International City Manager's Association referred to the city manager as a "community leader."[46] It was not long before city managers began to be told that they were the ones "most directly responsible to the public."[47] In accordance with this sentiment, professional publications emphasized the policy-making role of the municipal administrator, telling him (1) *how* to engage in policy formulation effectively[48] and (2), as if to compensate for the fallen idol of "neutral competence," *why* he should play a leading political role. In this respect, the "change agent" image was a timely arrival.[49]

The altruistic character of the city manager profession, long a matter of public record,[50] fit neatly the "change agent" image. However, by way of atonement for his over-attachment to the "conservative business community," the city manager in future "will have to become more of a human or social engineer" who cooperates with "social actionists" and who, on the basis of a "humanitarian social philosophy," employs his connection with the powerful in the cause of social justice.[51] He must "reach out" to help the "disadvantaged and concerned citizens of his city."[52]

A number of techniques have been developed for staging the "change agent" role in our administrative drama. Perhaps most important among these is the tactic of "leading through" elected bodies. For city managers, a most poignant statement on this matter comes from one, Steve Matthews.[53] Eschewing both the "neck manager" (one who takes it upon himself to make formal policy recommendations to the public) and the "fanny leader" (the manager who implements policies arrived at by elected officials), Matthews advocates a "manager who leads with his shoulders." Such a manager, Matthews continues, uses "salesmanship" in winning the city council and, through it, the public, to his point of view. "A manager should stay in the battleground," he writes, "he should push and lead through the council and the staff." Additionally, "ideas should be developed and shared with the council, giving them credit for good ones." In recruiting support among council members for his policies (or "their policies," depending on which side of the rabbit hole one prefers) the manager can reciprocate by briefing the council on anticipated questions and criticism from the public. In this regard, the use of private "study sessions" or "work sessions," through which the manager attempts to persuade the council to adopt his policy positions and to present them to the public in a united front, seems to enjoy a good deal of currency.[54] By controlling information and handling citizen complaints, "councilmen can be made to 'look good' or 'look bad' by the manager's systematic and shrewd utilization of his discretionary powers."[55] Additionally, the city manager is advised to use the leverage of both experts and citizens to convince elected officials of the soundness of his policies. As one city manager comments:

If I am trying to get a particular code, like a housing code, I have the expert, such as the building inspector, explain the code at a private meeting, then with the council's agreement, bring the matter up at the next city council meeting; and inasmuch as this is a controversial matter, ask the council to appoint a citizens [sic] committee to study the code. The citizens [sic] committee is likely to be influenced by the staff, and a broad foundation of public sentiment is developed.[56]

Although sometimes submerged in a formally representative body, administrative leadership often seems close enough to the surface of public scrutiny to require the attendant skill of "public relations." Indeed, this concern is no less reflected in private administration where the symbol of "business statesmanship" has become quite popular.[57] As Marion B. Folsom, a former Secretary of the Department of Health, Education and Welfare (and later, Chairman of Eastman Kodak) instructs:

> The progress of our nation's economy depends on a more widespread understanding of the role of business in our society, and on enthusiastic public support of those policies which will contribute to advances in business. The basis of such understanding and support depends, first, on the soundness of management actions, especially with regard to the broad public interest, and second, on management success in communicating the facts to the general public—in presenting them accurately and in an understandable way that can be readily identified with the public interest.[58]

Equally, among administrators in the public sphere, we find references to the "need" for "fostering an informed public,"[59] for "citizens' education" which will improve the image of the administrator in the eyes of the citizenry,[60] as well as specific techniques (such as "media relations" and the use of "citizens' committees") which are designed to bring this about.[61] Expanding "citizens' participation" is regarded as one of administration's objectives and we hear *(sans evidence)* that administrators are actually increasing "community participation" in the governing process.[62] It would be a mistake, however, to infer that actual, broad-based participation is a situation coveted by the administrator for its own sake (as opposed to *his* own sake). We noted, above, the ideology's tendency to value "professional" criteria over democratic ones in shaping policy decisions when the two sets of criteria came into conflict. It seems that when the ideology speaks of "democracy" or "participation" it has in mind much more the symbol than the substance of such. Regarding the experience of the 1960's at which time the Office of Economic Opportunity advanced the formula of "maximum feasible participation" for the disadvantaged clients of government, H. George Frederickson, for instance, observes that "most important[ly] . . . [this experiment] gave the residents of the ghetto at least the impression that they had the capacity to influence publicly made decisions that affected their well-being."[63]

The administrative processes of planning and budgeting have also been given a face-lift appropriate to the socially conscious, "change agent." The vocation of "advocacy planning," for example, "calls on planners to become spokesmen in the planning process for groups which are often thought to lack adequate advocates for their interests and views."[64] As such, planning is described as "almost pure democratic process."[65] Similarly, the Planning, Programming, Budgeting Systems (PPBS) approach to budgeting, which seeks to link the planning function of administration to the budgetary process, has been heralded as something of a booster shot for an ailing democracy.[66] Unless one bears in mind the distinction between symbols and substance, however, the tendency of PPBS to centralize power in administrative hands, while at the same time promoting democratic values, might appear to be contradictory. On the side of substance, a RAND Corporation (pioneers in PPBS) memorandum phrases the effects of adopting PPBS rather succinctly:

The entire operation must be the personal responsibility of the *executive head* of the organization. *No one at a lower level* has the authority or the right or the ability to acquire the knowledge required to perform the necessary tasks of coordination.[67]

A similar assessment might apply to a recent addition to the lore on budgeting as an instrument of democracy and social justice, something dubbed "needs-budgeting." As Bruce L. Gates has noticed, this budgeting tool both narrows the range of alternatives in budget decisions (by implying a conjunction between *existing* service technology and clientele groups), and permits the administrator, rather than the clientele, the definition of the "needs" themselves.[68] We should not overlook, however, the symbolic bonus accruing to administrators of this variety, as their occupations are embellished with the notion of "need" and its nuance of "helping."

Finally, the professional literature contains frequent references to social science as the means by which enlightened administrators can redeem democracy's promise. By becoming versed in the achievements of modern social science, the administrator is expected to improve his efforts "to help solve the problems of society" through "intelligent action and change [based on] scientific knowledge."[69] And this "scientific knowledge," we hear, has arrived none too soon. Faced with the growing turbulence and conflict of contemporary society, administrators will be able to reknit the rent fabric of society by promoting beneficial change and supplying more control in order to (paradoxically) protect freedom.[70] Proponents seem able to maintain this paradox by recourse to mechanistic models of society derived by the "general systems" approach. As one puts it: "Since social action normally involves a feedback loop, the socially controlled in some sense also control the controller; indeed, this is the major characteristic of political decision-making in a democracy."[71] In the "Space Age," perhaps "feedback loop" is a serviceable metaphor for citizenship.

Empirical Findings

The interviews conducted with American practitioners and academics provide some empirical grounding and some qualifications to the ideological tendencies which appear in the professional literature. As we noted in the previous chapter, those in the sample display a range of differences in their orientation toward the meaning or purpose of administration. Among those academics who tended to emphasize the eschatological dimension of administration (what we called "the ideology of signification"), administration was portrayed as an activity whose proper object is the perfection of the social order. There seemed no firm consensus, however, on what such perfection concretely implied. For some it appeared to mean knowledgeable, well-trained administrators "solving our most pressing problems." Others looked on the role of the administrator as that of a "change agent," underscoring his potential "to articulate the needs of those who have been left out of the political process" and "to build bridges between the government and those who most need the services of government."

Another group of academics, those employed in institutions providing primarily in-service training and/or part-time education to administrators, were taciturn on this matter. An unmistakable impression was conveyed during the interviews that for them the purpose of administration was more or less self-evident, namely, to administer. In this respect, at least, their outlook seemed quite close to the great majority of practitioners. A striking similarity in language also joins their perspectives. Not only did this sub-group of academics employ a "tough" language, a language characteristic of authority and one which discourages a critical orientation toward the political order,[72] but they tended to rely on the utility word "types" with a frequency at least equal to that of the practitioners. So, these academics often spoke of "academic types," "P.A. (public administration) types," etc. Focusing on this vernacular for a moment, it may be that this mode of expression is quintessentially "administrative." That is, the world "out there" is seen as being populated by standardized categories of people or "types." In the same way that administrative rationality, applied to work operations, is synonymous with increasing uniformity, predictability and routine, the perspective which the administrator adopts toward his environment appears to place a premium on these order-bringing attributes—hence, "types" is a preferred mode of expression. And just as the manipulation of the organization's personnel is facilitated by their categorization (superiors make decisions regarding "clerk-typists," for instance, not decisions which bear immediately on the individuals who happen to occupy clerk-typist positions), so the manipulation of the organization's environment proceeds along the same lines. People, in this respect, appear as "cases," as Weber noted,[73] or, as those in the sample seem to prefer, as "types."

When practitioners in the sample discussed the world in which they operated, they appeared to have in mind something which should be "run" according to "sound business practices" (an expression employed with considerable frequency). Regarding their relations with elected officials, many officials portrayed these as something of a nuisance. As one remarked: "We had to keep the [city] council updated on what's going on and try to work around the radicals." In this case, the "radicals" were two local businessmen in their mid-fifties who tended to be critical of the policies and procedures of the city manager's administration. For their part, the city councilmen in the sample evinced a feeling of being left out of the operations of government. This feeling, more or less intense, was uniform among those in the sample. Some typical comments illustrate it:

It takes at least a year (on the city council) to find out anything. The first year is pretty much a dead loss. You don't know what's going on. At meetings, you don't know what to say. You pretty much watch the city manager and his department heads run everything.

I wish there was some training for councilmen, we could sure use it. We would probably be a lot more effective in our job if we knew more about how to deal with problems.

We have to put our confidence in the city manager and the department heads.

The city manager and his subordinates try to run the city and cow the council into being a rubber stamp.

When practitioners spoke of the citizenry, their comments were at odds with those who emphasized the democratic potential of administration. The following remarks from administrators convey what seems to be a common orientation among the practitioners:

Government is something for people to take out their frustrations on.

The public either doesn't care or thinks we are wrong.

We don't have a chance to get our views to the public.

We never get much praise. People see failures not effort. I don't know if P.R. [public relations] would help or not.

These interviews left a consistent impression that administrators saw the public as an intrusion or a potential intrusion into a preserve that was rightly theirs. Some common remarks on this score:

If the community understood more what we're doing, they would be more tolerant.

City government should stay out of politics.

The city manager form of government is the only thing a city should have . . . [it] means better harmony.

Moreover, American administrators seemed to regard the local press about as highly as they did the general public. On no occasion did they speak of it in lauditory terms. Rather, when the topic was addressed, there followed such characterization as:

The paper here doesn't do enough in-perspective reporting.

Our paper gives us some constructive criticism but it is not experienced enough.

The newspaper is hostile to us.

Overall, the interviews with American administrators would suggest a picture of administration which is at odds with the democratic and participatory elements of the ideology. It seems much more consistent, on the other hand, with the obverse theme of government by professionals. And for such a government, society or the public can only be regarded as an object. When the public or parts of it act as subjects putting forward policy demands or criticisms, such is perceived, in the words of many in the sample, as a "problem." Public administration, we might infer, has come to depend for its *modus operandi* on an administered public. When the citizenry breaks with this expectation and takes upon itself an active role in political life, the normal routine of administration is also broken (hence, the "problem"). The ideology of administration lapses mute on this point. It appears to have no means of answering this problem inasmuch as the problem itself represents a direct challenge to what the ideology holds to be axiomatic, namely, government by administration.

7
Administrative Communism in the Soviet Union

In quite the same way as the idea of democracy in the United States has been reformulated by the exigencies of an administrative state, so the equivalent concept in the Soviet Union, "communism," has undergone a similar transformation. Likewise, a parallel obtains between the role ascribed to the administrative leader in either society. In the USSR, a veritable leadership cult has grown up around the person of the *rukovoditel'* which rivals in every respect the hero-like status which the American literature affords the administrative leader. Finally, bureaucracy for the Soviets has been embellished with representative and democratic characteristics. Despite the verbal salvos which issue ubiquitously in the USSR against something called "bureaucratism," the communist millenium is said to be present in embryo today in the form of modern administration.

This chapter surveys these three aspects of administrative ideology in the Soviet Union. Clearly, the aspects are integrally related; the maintenance of administration *after* the arrival of full communism, for example, implies the continuation of a special role and function for administrators who, in turn, require a special symbolic status to account for their position in the future. And since the future, "communism," is the ultimate legitimation for the extant political order, the symbology which surrounds the *rukovoditel'* is not without import in the present. In reconstructing the special ideology of administration which emanates from bureaucracy's external contradiction in the USSR, however, these three aspects of the ideology are treated separately for purposes of presentation. After surveying the professional literature, the discussion turns to some interview data which qualify the picture which emerges from the ideology's written expression.

Representative Bureaucracy in Soviet Garb

In Soviet administrative ideology, pride of place belongs to the Party. The Leninist variant of Marxian thought portrays the Party as "the vanguard of the proletariat" which acts, and perceives itself, as a surrogate for the revolutionary working class.[1] This inversion amounts to displacing the proletariat as the subject of revolution, transforming it into the object of the allegedly infallible "vanguard." As Trotsky remarked on the occasion of his demise at the Thirteenth Party Congress (1924):

The Party in the last analysis is always right because the Party is the single historic instrument given to the proletariat for the solution of its fundamental problems . . . I know that one must not be right against the Party. One can only be right with the Party, and through the Party, for history has created no other road for the realization of what is right.[2]

In similar fashion, contemporary Soviet writers claim that the Party leads "the entire life of Soviet society [through] scientifically based politics," that "the entire course of the Soviet socialist state shows that the soviets primarily need Communist guidance to bring out fully the tremendous advantages vouchsafed in Soviet government and their employment for the good of socialism."[3] The leading role of the Party derives its legitimation from two somewhat distinct sources. On the one hand, the Party has, purportedly, placed administration on a "scientific" footing.[4] Given its command of the "objective laws" of social development, the Party acts as the "conscious expressor of the objective historical process,"[5] which, through the perfection of the administrative apparatus, pushes society forward toward communism.[6] On the other, the Party's preeminent position in society is justified by democratic considerations. Democracy is somehow in the very "nature" of the Party.[7] And, with regard to its relationship to the society which it leads, the Party is depicted as the "mighty accumulator of the demands, strivings and creative experience of the popular masses, the mainspring of the entire mechanism of people's power."[8] Ideologues of this persuasion refer to it, therefore, as *"the mind, the honor and the conscience of our epoch,* of the Soviet people, realizing the great socialist transformation."[9]

Soviet ideology does not rest content, however, with claims of "scientific knowledge" *cum* "mind, honor and conscience" in characterizing the Party's role in society. Not only does the Party comprehend society's "objective laws," but "the most important natural law of the development of a socialist society is the growth of the leading role of the Communist Party" which asserts itself even more as communism is approached.[10] The Party's program, moreover, "has scientifically expressed not only the basic directions of development of our country, but also the general tendencies for the entire progressive development of mankind."[11] In this respect, the Party assumes a larger-than-life stature: the import of the system which it has built in the Soviet Union has world significance, as all humanity is destined to treat the Soviet path;[12] the Soviet Union, the cause of communism and the hope of a better future are, in official Soviet doctrine, equated.[13]

Enmeshed as it is in the day-to-day affairs of governing,[14] one might think that the Party would be vulnerable to the same feelings of frustration and the same sort of criticisms directed by Soviet citizens toward the system in general; namely, a lethargic, unresponsive bureaucracy and the waste and delays which such implies. Interestingly, the Party itself is forever registering such complaints. Here we find the argument made that somehow this system which the Party leads is a sluggish one, given to sinking into a state of torpor if the Party is not constantly on hand to spur it into activity. The Party has always resolutely endeavored to improve the administration of the state.[15] It has always fought against "bureaucratism" and on behalf of the workers vis-a-vis the bureaucracy.[16] As a bureaucratic organization itself, this line of "reasoning" has only been possible by means of a definition of bureaucracy which renders this phenomenon as nothing more than red tape and rote action. When the Party lashes out against bureaucratism in the state apparatus, it has in mind not the fact that this apparatus is bureaucratically structured, but the consideration that efficiency is suffering.[17]

The dominant role in Soviet political life played by administrative (whether Party of state) bodies is justified by essentially two claims:

(1) administration has a representative, democratic character itself and (2) administrative units are rather like islands in a sea of "socialist democracy," the lapping waves of which continually carry onto the shore of the state the direct participation of the citizenry. Regarding the first of these claims, the official designation of the USSR as a society which has progressed to the historical stage of "developed socialism" (an appellation first applied in the mid-seventies) and the adoption in 1977 of a new Soviet Constitution, merit brief comment. First, a certain, more or less explicit, depoliticization of public affairs has been on the rise in official Soviet commentary on the social changes symbolized by the new appellation and the new Constitution. In a developed socialist society, writes Leonid Volkov:

The state (as represented by its administrative bodies) and public organizations run both economic and public, cultural and other affairs. In this sense politics in various spheres of relations within a country should be treated as a component of management (in the broadest sense of the word), and the political behavior of social groups and individuals always has a managerial aspect.[18]

Volkov goes on to argue that increasing the discretion and decision-making latitude of top administration will "facilitate the democratic development of mature socialist society."[19] Administration, it would seem, is (like the Party) democratic in its very nature. According to other Soviet writers, the new Soviet Constitution captures this truth. This is precisely why, says Yu. A. Tikhomirov, the new Constitution has dropped the previous distinction between organs of power and organs of administration and why the legislative function of the latter has been expanded.[20]

Second, and in apparent juxtaposition to this tendency, the Soviet literature exhibits a redoubled effort to highlight the alleged participatory-democratic aspects of the Soviet state. This line of commentary tends to blur any distinction between state and society and to underline the supposed direct involvement of the population in deciding the crucial questions of politics and the superintending of the administrative apparatus. "Developed socialism," from this viewpoint, means that "the people themselves realize through the soviets the state power which belongs to them [the soviets], they [the people] administer the affairs of the state."[21] The dilemma posed by such a proposition—i.e., the potential rub between administration, based on "scientific and technical expertise," versus politics, grounded in mass participation—is not lost on the Soviets. Yet neither do their attempts to solve the dilemma amount to more than a leap from one of its horns to the other. That is, the scientific-technical character of administration is said to progress in tandem with its democratic-representative aspects inasmuch as more scientific and technical experts come to man the democratic-representative institutions.[22]

Finally, here, a word on a significant contrast between the American and Soviet variants of administrative ideology, a contrast which seems to be grounded in the respective structural differences which obtain between these two forms of modern industrialism. There is no counterpart in the American literature to the sweeping, and equally empty, generalizations found in Soviet writings with regard to the democratic involvement of the citizenry in the affairs of state or the heroic deeds performed on behalf of society by the people's representatives, the deputies of the soviets. In part, these peculiarly Soviet phenomena might be attributed to style and context. That is, a public sphere in which ideas contend would shape public statements in such a way that those arguments, so far removed from the obvious of everyday life as to warrant no credence, would hesitate to show their faces. In Soviet circumstances, a public sphere is, for all intents and purposes, absent. Hence, in this respect, any pronouncement is equivalent in its truth content to any other pronouncement. And, free to pronounce, the political leadership pronounces quite liberally. But the pronouncements do not seem intended to persuade. Their purpose is to define. For instance, Lazar Kaganovich, once remarked with regard to municipal affairs, that "a socialist city is a city in the Soviet Union."[23] This statement, perhaps as well as any other, illustrates the phenomenon in question. The idea of socialism is defined by what exists in the USSR, and what exists is, correspondingly, "socialism." One would be hard pressed to show that Soviet style has in any appreciable way changed since Kaganovich's time.

Yet, another, not unrelated but more deeply rooted, reason for the observable differences between the respective American and Soviet literatures on this count would be the depoliticizing influence of the market in the US and what we earlier termed "the illusory politicization of the public sphere" as a form of class domination in the USSR.

The appearance of a political life is a ubiquitous phenomenon in the Soviet Union—assemblies, meetings, speeches, demonstrations, placards, and so forth. Millions on millions are involved in one form or another of ostensibly political activity—deputies of soviets, activists, members of self-managing cooperatives, social organizations. Why? We have noted already the directly political character of class domination in the USSR, a phenomenon which depends heavily on coercion, state censorship and this "illusory politicization" which pivots on the official definition of reality. Here, we might add the particular relation which all of this bears to the enterprise of securing a "representative" character for politically dominant administrative bodies. Namely, administrative power is enfolded with layer on layer of pseudo-democratic elements—the deputies, activists, volunteers and so on. In and of themselves, these elements are politically impotent. Any power to be realized can only be realized through the existing powers—administrative bodies. Yet, the presence of these pseudo-democratic elements is not unimportant for the legitimation of administrative power before society, for when the average citizen confronts the state he is most often confronting his deputy or the activists in his place of work or residence. The appearance, then, is one of popular government. Should one question the authenticity of such, one has thereby excommunicated oneself from public discussion. The pronouncement of reality is, like Kaganovich's "socialist city," equivalent to the reality of the pronouncement. Soviet statements on the representative nature of administration are, in this odd way, "true"—not because they seek to persuade their audience, nor because they conform to what one might perceive in the world. They are true because they define what does or does not exist and true because there are no competing definitions.

Administrators and Leadership

As is true of the American literature on administration, there is a widespread acknowledgement among Soviet writers that administrators make decisions. B. D. Lebin and M. N. Perfil'ev put it like this:

In a number of cases [administrators are in a situation in which no] representative organs have made the decisions, nor have the planners. It is natural, that in these situations the organizational activity of the cadres of the apparatus of administration is not discontinued. Included within the organizational cycle of administrative labor are attempts to find (coming out of their own knowledge, experience, intuition) the best decision. It appears to us, that such type of activity on the part of the cadres of the apparatus of administration is necessary and may be considered as one of the elements of organizational activity.[24]

With a slightly different emphasis, Popkov has said that the administrator "must make an autonomous decision within the framework of the law, he must find the most expedient approach to the matter."[25] Yet, L. A. Sergienko and A. S. Kokovin have argued that this framework may be elastic. The administrator, in their view, has a "creative relationship" with legal acts, interpreting and implementing them not "mechanically," but "consciously" in accord with both the requirements of the law and those of the present day. Hence, the administrator and the law form "an organic unity."[26] However mystical may be this relationship between the administrator and the law, it is clear that the making of decisions is "the most important act of administration,"[27] that such decisions have themselves the force of law,[28] and administrative cadres are therefore regarded as "the directors" of society.[29]

As to why it is the administrator who should occupy this position, Soviet ideology abounds with justifications. To begin with the more mundane arguments, administrators decide social questions because they hold the keys which unlock the mysteries of social life, the "objective laws" of social development. In this context, we find:

Talented *rukovoditeli*, in the course of mastering their professions, scientifically approach the decisions or problems of the administration of social processes, deeply study the natural laws of their development and the practical experience of the people, realistically evaluate the achieved results, critically approach the shortcomings and see the perspectives of the movement forward, striving to find the most effective means of quickening social progress.[30]

This alleged ability to "get results" has prompted one Soviet writer to claim that the Soviet Union was able to weather the first stormy years of its existence "primarily as a result of skilled management."[31] We can note, in this respect, a cult of expertise which finds expression in a manner identical to that of its counterpart in the

United States, viz., "professionalism." "One of the most distinctive qualities of the civil service," says Yu. A. Tikhomirov:

is the organization of their [i.e., the civil servants'] work on the basis of professionalism. Many objective factors (political, economic, organizational, legal, technical, psychological) require the creation of a stable and qualified personnel of the state organs. . . . Hence, a specialization of the functions of administration must be deduced, requiring special knowledge and practice. . . . Therefore, the entire people, who hold power entrust to a specific category of workers the fulfillment of the function of administration.[32]

But *rukovoditeli* hold their trust by virtue of more than "talent" and "professionalism." Their professional ethics are said to breed a high "moral conscience" among the administrative stratum.[33] They have a "socially necessary function" to fulfill in coordinating the work of others (because of the division of labor)[34] and this function is performed with all the trappings of eschatology. Sometimes we find the eschatological running in tandem with the mundane. Popkov writes that "honor" is "mutually connected with achievement," they appear "as a single social-ethical entity."[35] Similarly, I. L. Bachilo lists "the qualities of *rukovodeiteli*" as "political maturity, specialized knowledge, administrative experience, and a virtuous character."[36] At other times, however, the eschatological element seems almost to stand on its own. Examples would include the emphasis placed on the allegedly high moral character of *rukovoditeli*,[37] their profound sensitivity to the needs and aspirations of others.[38] A related matter, here, is the political vision of the *rukovoditel'*, his capacity to not only take the correct action but to simultaneously edify others in the process, raising thereby their political consciousness.[39] In this regard, "the moral qualities of a worker supplement his political qualities."[40] Together, these attributes entitle *rukovoditeli* to act as "examples" for those in their charge,[41] and before the entire society.[42]

In addition to being "examples," the title "representatives" is also conferred upon *rukovoditeli*.[43] This appellation does not depend on any concretia, such as elections (even Soviet-style elections). "If election," say Lebin and Perfil'ev, "might entail a lowering of the level of competence and authority of the *rukovoditel'* or the *ispolnitel'* (executive), then it cannot be a preferred method of forming the apparatus of the executive-managerial organs in all cases."[44] Rather, it is through their efforts in solving society's problems that *rukovodi-teli* "cultivate a feeling of civic responsibility for their own work, which is the basis of the self-awareness of the civil servant as an executor of the will of the workers."[45] As such, *rukovoditeli* are held to serve directly the interests of the working class, in particular, and the entire society, in general.[46] By definition, again there can be no distinction between administrative and social interests, for:

In the conditions of the Soviet order, the activity of the state apparatus serves the interests of the laborers and is directed toward the construction of communism—the most humane and just social order.[47]

The intelligentsia (and, of course, *rukovoditeli* as members of this stratum) "lives as one in interest with all toilers."[48] As V. S. Semenov has opined:

In the factories, construction sites, enterprises, in the kolkhozes and sov-khozes, the intelligentsia and civil servants are toiling side by side, shoul-der to shoulder with the workers and peasants.[49]

Finally, the matter of popular participation in the affairs of the state takes on a slightly different tone when considered from the viewpoint of the administrative leader himself. The *rukovoditel'* is responsible for "the task of attracting all citizens to the administra-tive affairs of society,"[50] and thereby, "to stimulate the development of their political activity" and to nuture "the all-around develop-ment of the individual" such that the public self "becomes part of the spiritual life of the individual which he consciously implements in life."[51] As T. H. Rigby has pointed out, the name given to this process, the "mobilization of the masses," is equivalent to the Amer-ican term, "public relations," and amounts to a means by which decisions reached at the top are "sold" to the larger society.[52] Hence, the *rukovoditel'* is instructed to act as a "constant agitator"[53] in the cause of "communist construction," itself a shibboleth for "the ability to administer."[54]

Redefining "Communism"

Administrative ideology in the Soviet Union has not been particu-larly kind to the philosophy of Karl Marx. The idea of communism and its redefinition in that country point up the repeated raids made by administrative thought on the larder of official truth. Many of this larder's contents have been appropriated to the administrative purpose; what is replaced are often empty casings. Three aspects of Marx's idea of communism, and their negation in Soviet administrative ideology, merit particular attention. These are: (1) the possibility of a state, contrary to Marx, existing in the communist future; (2) the maintenance of a division of labor, again *contra* Marx, under communism, and (3) the continuation of administration (and Engels comes in for it, here) in a communist society.

Stalin's "theory" of "socialism in one country" might be seen as the cornerstone for the present Soviet "theory" of the state and as a central feature of Soviet Marxism. Clearly, the doctrine was tailored to the practical purposes of "getting on with" the business of industrializing the USSR in the absence of successful revolutions in western countries, giving thereby a certain "positive direction" or rationale to state action. But its ramifications extend beyond these simple considerations.

As Marcuse has shown, the doctrine of "socialism in one country" solves the external and internal contradictions of the Soviet Union by elevating the directing role of the state over society and justifying the state's repressive functions.[55] The ideology of Stalinism, as voiced by P. F. Yudin, claims that "strengthening the Soviet state . . . is the main task of present as well as future activity in the construction of a communist society."[56] Stalin himself remarked at the Eighteenth Party Congress (1939) that the state will remain even in a communist society if the "hostile capitalist encirclement" has not ended.[57] In a word, "socialism in one country" amounts to an anti-revolutionary perspective; that is, the state is elevated to the position of conscious director of society, and political thought becomes a by-product of its needs. As Marcuse, again, has suggested, thought thereby becomes non-transcendent. In art, for instance, the slogan of "socialist realism" is raised; but this brand of realism does not show the ideal in its actual negation—rather, it portrays reality as the ideal come to fruition.[58] This movement in artistic thought, the ideal portrayed as reality, might be understood as the counterbalancing movement to Soviet statism wherein reality is regarded as the ideal.

In current Soviet writings, many of the same themes are repeated. According to pronouncement, the state "expresses the interests and will of all classes and social groups of our society."[59] There is here a principle of "constant and complete correspondence of the state service to the will and interests of the Soviet people," a principle which "directly flows out of the very essence of Soviet power as a state created by the workers and for the workers."[60] Despite such populist rhetoric, however, it is the state which is regarded as "the subject of administration" and society is its corresponding "object."[61] Given that the Soviets claim the mantle of orthodox Marxism and that Marx foresaw a stateless society under communism, the question of resolving the apparent contradiction between Marx's writings and the continued existence of a state has given rise to no small number of emendations and equivocations in the Soviet literature on this topic. Khrushchev, for example, came up with the idea of an "all-people's state," a notion which signified that in the Soviet Union, where socialism had been built and class conflict has ceased, an historically new type of state has arisen, i.e., one which did not represent, as had the previous "dictatorship of the proletariat," the rule of one class over another. The problem here, of course, is obvious; for Marx, all states are the products of antagonistic class relationships and all states, therefore, represent class rule. Khrushchev's innovation seems to have faded from fashion after his own political demise,[62] only to be revived again in the mid-seventies as the governmental counterpart to the officially proclaimed society of "developed socialism."[63] The precise relationship of the state to the question of social classes, however, remains somewhat enigmatic. K. F. Sheremet, for instance, has argued that the task of strengthening the Soviet state is fully congruent with the extension of democracy, inasmuch as this is *not* a state formed out of class relations but one whose function is the expression of a popular will.[64] However, only ten months prior to the publication of these thoughts, the same author made quite clearly the counter-argument, opining that the Soviet state has not lost its "class-proletarian essence" because there is "no supraclass democracy."[65] That a given author might reverse his views on some topic is beside the point. Of import, here, is the fact that each of these conflicting statements on a matter of considerable doctrinal significance received the impramatur of the state censor. The larder is, indeed, depleted. Accordingly, when one reads that there is "no sharp distinction" between the "dictatorship of the proletariat" and the "all-people's state," it comes as no surprise to find that the author neglects to mention any distinctions whatsoever.[66]

A certain accommodation to the present order is no less evident in the work of Soviet writers who emphasize the temporary nature of the state. V. M. Manokhin, for one, writes that the withering of the state and the concomitant end of administration as a special profession do not imply that state service is any less important for the building of communism in the immediate future.[67] Indeed, on the road to communism the state apparatus must be strengthened,[68] and, with it, "conscious discipline" and "strict order" are maintained; "the functions of the leadership of the economy, the social and cultural life of the country, which in the present time are realized by the state, are preserved in the conditions of communism."[69]

The political aspects of "communist construction" bear two striking similarities to the American variant of administrative ideology. First, for democracy and citizenship, the ideology substitutes "feedback";[70] citizen participation is reduced to a practice by which the state takes popular opinion into account in formulating policy.[71] Second, considerable attention is given to the internalization of social duty by the "New Soviet Man," a theme which recalls Drucker's idea of management by objectives which "substitutes for control from the outside the stricter more exacting and more effective control from the inside." Here, the communist education of the "New Man" is supposed to take account of human needs. But not just any needs; rather, "reasonable and healthy needs" such as "the need for work and knowledge."[72] By properly molding this needs-structure, it is believed that unconscious habit will soon have society on the prescribed track and the conscious regulation of man's activities by the state will become superfluous. It is in this sense, then, that the state is to wither away. Yet insofar as this withering is to take place, we find that it is an administratively directed process.

The development of responsibility by the leading cadres of the Soviet state apparatus acquires a particularly important significance in contemporary conditions, for they, in the first place, must set an example in the discipline of labor, in the working out and realization of the most effective decisions. Their behavior in the social plan has value not only in the plan of objective material results, but also in a moral aspect, with the account of the influence of their behavior or the formation of the moral features of the Soviet people.[73]

As with the question of the state, Soviet writers have effected a redefinition of the division of labor and its abolition in two ways.

First, the division of labor has been reduced to be the division between "mental" and "manual" work.[74] Consequently, it is claimed that as technology becomes more sophisticated, the sphere of manual labor will progressively shrink until all workers are finally "mental" workers. This leaves intact, however, the fact of specialization, i.e., individuals performing segmented functions in the economy. Specialization is the second Soviet reinterpretation. Karpushin rather scholastically renders specialization as that occurring among the "subjects" of labor (that is, those who perform the work) and claims that since specialization will obviously continue under communism, it cannot be understood as a division of labor.[75] Afanas'ev, on the other hand, asserts that the division of labor can be overcome through *more* professional specialization, coupled with more general-science education.[76]

Afanas'ev has also provided a remarkable characterization of leisure time in the new society. He cautions against its abuse by those with:

a passion for liquor, drawn out sessions of playing dominoes, cards and other pointless pass-times. Time is money, they said in the old days. In our time, we can say that time, in particular free time, is dearer than money, even, that by uselessly wasting free time man robs himself and impoverishes himself spiritually and physically.[77]

Consequently, like any other productive resource, free time is to be put to "effective use," primarily by enrolling in courses of study related to work.[78]

Finally, regarding the place of administration in the future communist society, Soviet writers have come up with some no less remarkable emendations to the original Marxian conception. The least imaginative among these simply see communism as the perfection of the present order; administrative functions remain but are (needless to say, quite gradually) transferred to social organizations.[79] For this group, administration remains a long-term prospect, as the all-important scientific-technological revolution "can successfully develop *only in conditions of the rational regulation of social relations*,"[80] meaning that, although social organizations take on some tasks, "the state preserves for itself the 'commanding heights.' "[81] A second group feels that under communism administration will itself become automated.[82] This seems very close to a revision of Engels' famous dictum, whereby communism is redefined not as the administration "of" things, but the administration "by" things.[83] A third group would unabashedly retire Engels' pronouncement altogether. "The words of F. Engels, that under communism the administration of people will be replaced by administration of things, cannot be taken literally. A communist society is unthinkable without the regulation of the activity of people."[84]

Empirical Findings

The interviews conducted with Soviet practitioners and academics tend to support in general the main outlines of administrative ideology's response to the external contradiction. As was the case with their American counterparts, the data additionally point up some differences in perspective and emphasis between practitioners and academics in the USSR. The ideology appears to be received and fashioned in a manner peculiar to each of the respective groups; in some respects Soviet academics, for example, seemed closer in their outlook to American academics than to practitioners of their own country.

Although a few minutes of each interview would ordinarily be given over to enumerating the ways in which (on paper) Soviet democracy has surpassed the bourgeois variety, the conception of "democracy" for both academics and practitioners appeared to mean something akin to popular consent. To be sure, academics were often quick to criticize what they saw as shortcomings in the political system, at least in a general way, and to express confidence regarding the possibilities for citizen participation in the political process in the future. As one candidly stated:

The question of bringing the masses into the administration of affairs has really only been solved in an economic sense. Politically, very little has been done. There are exceptions, of course, such as the popular discussion of draft legislation or opinion surveys. But in the main it can be said that the masses are not politically involved to a great degree.

Although supportive in principle of the idea of direct popular involvement in government, academics often tended to reduce the concept of democracy to that of popular consent. For instance:

Clearly, the most important forms of popular democracy in the Soviet Union today are the influence of public opinion on the government and political prognosis. These forms compensate for the absence of other democratic institutions.

Practitioners, for their part, seemed to interpret "democracy" as the "satisfying of the population's needs." The difference between these two groups in their respective interpretations of "democracy" appears quite small at first. Each seems a variation on the idea of democracy as popular consent; each, to some degree, would imply the other. Hence, it can be said that the empirical evidence does ground the "reduction of democracy" specified by the ideal type. Yet it should be added that the difference which does obtain appears consistently in the comments of each group regarding their characterizations and evaluations of the various institutions and practices contained in the idea, "Soviet democracy." We can apply our terms "ideology of results" and "ideology of signification" to these outlooks and illustrate their differences by looking at the comments made by practitioners and academics on two topical areas, the electoral system (broadly conceived) and the role of social organizations.

Academics tended to stress formal improvements in the electoral system, portraying these as important advances for democracy in the USSR. Regarding the nomination of candidates, for example, one pointed out that:

The process has been greatly improved. Not many years ago not social organizations but their [administrative] organs in fact nominated deputies. That is not democratic, these are, after all, organs, local organs, maybe, but *organs* all the same. Now, conferences of the whole organization carry out the nominating process.

On the other hand, deputies whom I interviewed attached little significance to the democratic aspects of the nominating procedure or the relationship between themselves as deputies and the organization which nominated them. One deputy, speaking of the reports which he delivers to his constituents, mentioned his annual report before his nominating organization more or less as an afterthought. Another remarked:

Tomorrow I go to report to my nominating organization. It has been two years since they nominated me. It [the report] is really a formality. I don't know them, they don't know me.

The same difference marked the evaluation of each group regarding the annual or (depending on the locale) semi-annual report of the deputy to his constituents. Academics laid considerable emphasis on the fact that effectively all deputies in the USSR now fulfill this obligation before the electorate and that the frequency of reports (twice per year in some places) has increased. Deputies, however, seemed less sanguine, as these comments from two of them show:

In this district, all the deputies report regularly to their constituents. Unfortunately, not many people attend these meetings.

[When I report to my constituents] these meetings are well attended, but almost all the people who come are older. One would like to see more young people there. I suppose that it is the problem of a big city. In smaller towns it is easy to organize such participation. In (this city), however, there is more to do and young people go out to other things.

It should be added, here, that "objectively," so to speak, there may be very little at stake in these meetings in the constituency, for their importance, from the point of view of democracy, would be predicated upon the ability of the electorate to hold their deputy responsible. Since election itself is a foregone conclusion, the nominating and renominating process would figure heavily in holding one's representative accountable for his actions. Yet, this procedure itself seems to be administratively orchestrated. As election time approaches, the members of various executive committees told me, social organizations are advised by the executive committee of the soviet in question as to whether their candidate last time around should be renominated.

The election itself was characterized somewhat differently. Academics placed particular emphasis on two features of the election process as they understood it. First, its "collectivist" character. As one remarked: "In elections, the individual does not participate as an individual but as a member of a social organization."

Second, the giving of *nakazy* by the constituents to their candidate ("*nakazy*" are instructions which stand somewhere between demands and requests) during the campaign period. Academics viewed this practice as an outstanding example of popular democracy. Although most saw room for improvement, they were of one mind in attaching great import to the democratic features of this institution.

Practitioners, however, paid less attention to each of these, and, insofar as they mentioned them at all, tended to bring out other, more mundane aspects of the election and *nakaz* process. Elections, at least in part, seem to give Soviet officials the opportunity to periodically check the political pulse of their respective constituencies. Ironically, the pulse is registered not by voting, but by staying away from the polling place. As one told me:

I think that participation in the last election in our district was very high, about 99.8 or 99.9 per cent. We think it is important, however, to know why the few who did not vote stayed away. In one case, a man was angry because some repair work on his apartment had not been done. He told us: "No repair, no vote." In another case, some (religious sect) stayed away. That is a matter of faith. Well, what can you say? In a third, some trouble on the street with hooligans made a woman, who had in fact been on her way to the polls, quite unhappy. "With streets like these," she told us, "why should I vote for you."

Such "pulse taking" seems uppermost in the minds of practitioners when they discuss the role of the deputy. Whereas academics tend to portray the deputy as a tribune who carries the interests of his constituents into the decision-making arena, practitioners prefer to think of the deputy as a monitor of the popular mood, as a "signal to us," as a sort of emissary *to* the citizenry. The institution of the deputies' group (a number of deputies who reside in the same housing complex or who work in the same enterprise) is valued for this: "Deputies' groups reflect the opinions of the working class. They are channels of information for us."

On the other side of the coin, the deputy is valued for his role in what might be called public relations. As one practitioner put it:

Some pensioners are a real problem here. They make a request which we cannot fulfill at this time or some request which is just ridiculous. And they don't stop. They write us letters, they come on reception day, they write letters to the newspapers. In such cases the deputy will visit these people and convince them of the unjust nature of their requests, showing them the facts of the matter.

The emphasis which academics placed on the deputy's role of "tribune" found no resonance among the practitioners in the sample. Just the reverse. In this respect the soviet seems more than "a school of administration," as the phrase appears in the Soviet lexicon; it is also something of a socialization process which accustoms the deputy to "the state view." One practitioner commented that:

> When a new deputy speaks at the first session, it happens that nobody knows what he is talking about. After a year, however, he is a "state man" and his comments are better informed.

These contrasting views of academics and practitioners regarding the role of the deputy seem related to a larger issue, namely, the nature of the link between population and government. The ideology of signification employed by academics tends to emphasize the democratic aspects of this link. Over the course of the interviews, a strong impression was conveyed by academics that they valued popular pressures on government, public controversy over policy questions and the like. Practitioners, as might be expected, tended to view these things as "problems," as unstable elements in their environment, as impediments to getting results. They therefore prized tranquility. The matter of the press illustrates as well as any other this difference. Academics pointed with pride to the existence in some districts of a local newspaper which carried local news and contained criticism and suggestions from the citizenry itself. Such a practice, they explained, raised issues, raised controversy, raised popular consciousness and the level of popular involvement in government. Practitioners, however, took a different view. Of those interviewed, not one mentioned a local paper. When asked if such would be a desirable addition to the locality, they all responded in the negative—"not necessary." One practitioner was a bit more candid in this reply:

> Where I used to work there was such a local paper. We would all rush into the office and read it. A sense of relief would come over us—[smile] there's nothing about us today.

In the manner of American administrators, then, those in the Soviet sample seem to regard democratic action as a "problem" in their environment. Ironically, the administered democracy practiced in that country brings with it its own problems and *it is these* which tend to occupy the minds of practitioners. Academics, on the other hand, are not beset by this variety of difficulty, and tend therefore to focus on questions of another order, questions of democracy (or, often, its relative absence). What is at issue here might be illustrated by a quite ordinary problem faced by Soviet officials who administer the election process. One such recounted her experience in this way:

I was responsible for the vote [i.e., the turnout of voters] in my housing block. I had a few people working under me, each of whom was responsible for seeing to it that every person voted. Our goal was 100 per cent. Well, everything seemed to be going well and then, late in the afternoon, I received word from one of my subordinates that two old women in his sector had refused to go to vote. I rushed right over. "What is the matter?" I asked them. Each accused the other of dirtying the room [which they shared]. Each explained to me that she was not about to vote for a government which assigned her to a room shared by such a disgusting person. "Ladies," I said, "this is, after all, election day. This is an important matter. Can we let a dirty floor stand in the way of our duty to vote?" They would not budge. So I myself, yes, I myself went for the bucket and soap. I got down on my knees and I scrubbed that floor. Such is the nature of work with the public.

The richness in this recitation is unmatched by the stilted prose of Soviet ideology. Its closeness to life is a feature which sets it apart from the abstract ruminations of academics. But, most importantly, this account seems to shed some light on the differences which we have found in the interview sample between practitioners and academics in each country. To some degree, each group appears to be preoccupied with a different issue: signification draws the attention of the academic, the perspective of the practitioner is fixed on results. Such a divergence implies a certain split in the ideology or, at least, a split between two groups, each emphasizing different elements of the ideology. The implications of this split involve, on reflection, certain general features of administration and its attendant ideology, a topic which is addressed in the following chapter.

8
Conclusions and Implications

It remains, here, to review briefly and to summarize the main outlines of the argument presented in this study. Additionally, a certain amount of speculation might be in order with regard to situating and interpreting the ideology of administration within administration's practical context. In this respect, the divergences which emerged in the interview data between academics and practitioners invite comment. First, in schematic form, the summary.

1. Administrative ideology, at the most general level, conceives the practice of modern administration as bringing to human affairs a "rational" form of organization, for which is claimed the maximization of productive results through the most "effective" and "efficient" utilization of a "neutral" technology. At this level, the ideology fashions a legitimation for the uneven distribution of power within a bureaucratic hierarchy and for the class divisions which stand behind and are mediated by it. The legitimation, drawing upon notions attributed to the natural sciences, seeks to naturalize the social and political circumstances of bureaucracy. More precisely, the members of a bureaucratic system (people) are comprehended in administrative thought in a manner analogous to that of natural science vis-a-vis nature, as quantitative entities (things) devoid of qualitative content which admit, thereby, to comparison, one to another, and which can, therefore, be combined, coordinated and directed in the most "rational" (cost/benefit) manner by those at the apex of the structure (the administrative "generalist"). Consequently, bureaucracy, a domination structure, appears in administrative ideology as a technical necessity (in order to coordinate the sub-divided tasks), as a "rational" organizational

125

arrangement suited to the accomplishment of "collective" purposes. The exercise of power by those in command of a bureaucracy is, as a result, transformed from a political category into a technical one.

2. The general categories through which administrative ideology is expressed are hypostatized attributes of a reification, "the organization." These attributes, "efficiency" and "effectiveness," are the appearances manifest to those at the top of the bureaucratic hierarchy; viewed from the bottom, these terms connote, respectively, the alienation and subdivision of labor. In Chapter Three, we subjected these to a dialectical treatment and found (a) that each category, as the ideology would have it, is mutually dependent on and defined by the other and (b) that each contains within itself a contradiction with respect to its implications for the organization, on the one hand, and its individual members, on the other. This second conclusion is something which the ideological categories conceal, given their one-sided comprehension of administrative practice. To conceal, however, is not to remove, and as a result the contradictions contained in thought seek further resolution. In the same way, the *practice* of administration guided by these categories involves an internal contradiction (that springing from the limits of the administrator's formal authority which he goes beyond or seeks to overcome without undercutting this same authority) and an external contradiction (involving the incongruity between the formal norms of democracy in each of the two societies and the actual political dominance of bureaucratic bodies in the political process). Consequently, "special" ideologies of administration, addressing themselves to these contradictions, have developed and their appearances in the US and USSR take quite similar forms.

3. The "special" ideologies of administration cannot be directly derived from the "general" one, owing to the contradictions within it. Indeed, were there conformity between the general ideology and administrative practice itself, the special ideologies would not, so to speak, be "needed." Nonetheless, each contains a myriad of elements, images, etc., which are at home with the general ideology of modern administration, elements such as "expertise," "competence" and "professionalism." These have here been called the "mundane" side of administrative ideology. Additionally, we have spoken of an "eschatological" side in reference to a plethora of

claims found in the professional literature which highlight the alleged moral and altruistic qualities of administrators, portraying them as "self-actualizers" of their subordinates and "guardians" of the public interest. For the special ideology generated by the internal contradiction, the dominant theme seems to be "creative leadership." In sum, it amounts to a symbolic justification which supplements the formal authority of the administrator with a personal claim to leadership, and provides him with a collection of tools designed to effect a "creative" posture and to secure, thereby, improved organizational performance. The ideological reflection of the external contradiction also leans heavily on self-styled conceptions of "leadership" and explains to administrators why they do (they are the only ones with the requisite competence) and should (they are of superior moral calibre) make decisions for society. In order to harmonize the administrator's decision making role with the normative context extant in each country, the normative context has been itself redefined. In the United States, we find that "democracy" has surrendered to the claim of "realism." Administrative direction flows from the need for "competence." Yet this competence is purportedly of the enlightened, public-spirited variety which takes the part of the disadvantaged and promotes, thereby, democratic "values" (as opposed to democratic action). The notion of "communism" in the Soviet Union has been similarly reinterpreted. While it remains the linchpin of the eschatology, the Marxian understanding of the terms has been shunted aside, leaving a symbolic shell which contains administrative desiderata (the maintenance of a state, the continuation of a division of labor in society, the preservation of administration as a special function).

4. The results of interviews conducted with American and Soviet practitioners and academics suggest (a) that the concept of administrative ideology as abstracted from the professional literature is well-grounded empirically for the sample as a whole, but (b) these two groups are divided by their perceptions and evaluations of administration into those who emphasize "signification" (academics) and those concerned with "results" (practitioners).

Turning to the implications of this study, we might put directly the question of ideology's function in the social world. If ideology captures, transforms and symbolically resolves contradictions in social life, it must concomitantly compel belief in its propositions in order to affect or stabilize contradictory social practice. Does the ideology of administration compel belief? When measured against the status of myth in traditional society or the ideology of "fair exchange" in classical capitalism, the answer is perforce: No, not really. Unlike its predecessors, administrative ideology is more a product of conscious manufacture, more transparent in design, more contradictory in its internal make up. Hence, some observers have concluded that administration is incapable of generating legitimations for the present order and that this order is consequently in a state of crisis.[1] Others have seen this relative absence of convincing legitimation as a generalized lack of committment in and to the prevailing order, a lack of commitment which constitutes certain "weak spots" in the domination system.[2] My own assessment is that, although insightful with respect to certain changes brought on by modern industrialism, these observations miss the point. That is, they seem to be judging the present by the standards of the past, standards which may no longer serve adequately because the social formations from which they derive have been superseded by a new ordering with new forms of power.

To put the shoe on the other foot, we might for argument's sake entertain the idea that these "weak spots" are instead the forte of administrative power and its attendant ideology. If, for example, administrative ideology were a logically consistent system of propositions, if it compelled belief, such would represent an immanent limit to the use of administrative power. Administrative transgressions of administrative rules, for instance, could be challenged on the basis of the rules themselves. In the same way, the principles behind a given legitimation could serve the argument against he legitimation. (For example, if we are actually trying to promote "efficiency," how can this practice—say, limiting foreign competition in the American auto market or engaging in wasteful practices to meet planned output targets in the Soviet Union—be justified?) More, acting in opposition to its own legitimation structure, administration would be continually de-legitimating itself. However, what if the world were a bit closer to that described by Kafka? What if the rules themselves were constantly changing? What if the (inconsistent) principles were varied enough as to offer "explanations" (never mind good ones) for a wide range of decisions and directives? It seems to me that this type of ideology is congruent with administration in the modern world, for in this world the bases from which power, if not legitimate, might be challenged have been largely removed. Without control of their work and their craft, those within organizations have precious little ground from which to offer resistance to those in authority. Without a public life and an active public sphere, (active) citizens slide quite quickly into the status of (passive) consumers.

This aspect of administrative ideology, its weakness in compelling belief, seems to surface in the differences between practitioners and academics in the interview sample. Certainly, the differences are in part due to the relative position of each group in what Colin Sumner has called "the institutions of ideology maintenance and development."[3] The academics in the sample, the group most involved with such institutions, tended to exhibit in their oral statements a much greater affinity to the ideology's eschatological elements, elements which are quite pronounced in the professional literature. Although practitioners seemed much more interested in "results" than in "signification," it may be an error to dismiss the relevance of signification for them. That is, although not uppermost in their consciousness, this side of the ideology may act something like background or mood music setting a comfortable tone, constituting a comforting presence but not establishing any manifest injunctions. Injunctions derive more from the exigencies of power in the milieu in which they operate. To listen too attentively to the music may well take their minds from the work before them.

In sum, the ideology of administration differs from classical capitalist ideology in a more profound way than its relative failure to compel belief. For such belief makes always vulnerable a given institution on its own terms.[4] Administrative ideology does not appear to share this liability. As soon as the argument is joined on certain grounds, the grounds can be shifted. In this regard, the ideology of administration succeeds as an ideology for administration. It is not defensible in the face of abstract or reasonable standards. It is not about "rationality," "efficiency" and "effectiveness" in general; its concern is with these properties as mediated by administration as a system of power. It is in this regard, on its own terms, that the import of the ideology of administration must be measured.

Notes

Preface

1. Max Horkheimer, *Critical Theory* (New York: Herder and Herder, 1972), p. 7.
2. Colin Sumner, *Reading Ideologies* (London: Academic Press, 1979), p. 63.
3. For a full discussion of this point, see Alfred Schutz's "Concept and Theory Formation in the Social Sciences," *The Journal of Philosophy*, vol. 51 (1954); idem, "Some Leading Concepts in Phenomenology," *Social Research*, vol. 12 (February 1945).
4. H. H. Gerth and C. Wright Mills, eds., *From Max Weber: Essays in Sociology* (New York: Oxford University Press, 1946), pp. 196-244 (hereafter cited as *Weber.*)

1. Administrative Ideology: Concept and Method

1. Karl Marx, "Theses on Feuerbach," *Karl Marx and Frederick Engles Selected Works* (Moscow: Progress, 1968), p. 28.
2. For examples of this usage of the term, a usage with which the present study has little in common, see Giovanni Sartori, "Politics, Ideology, and Belief Systems," *American Political Science Review*, vol. 65 (September 1971). The so-called "end of ideology" debate was largely framed around this understanding of the term "ideology." See, in particular, Daniel Bell, *The End of Ideology* (New York: The Free Press, 1962).
3. Anthony Downs, *Inside Bureaucracy* (Boston: Little Brown and Co., 1967) pp. 223-243; esp. p. 237.
4. I have in mind here such authors as Samuel A. Stouffer, "Some Observations on Study Design," *American Journal of Sociology*, vol. 55 (June 1950); Robert K. Merton, *Social Theory and Social Structure* (rev. ed., Glencoe, Ill.: The Free Press, 1957); Giovanni Sartori, "Concept Misformation in Comparative Politics," *American Political Science Review*, vol. 64 (December 1970); Adam Przeworski and Henry Teune, *The Logic of Comparative Social Inquiry* (New York: Wiley-Interscience, 1970); Abraham Kaplan, *The Conduct*

131

of *Inquiry* (Scranton, Pa.: Chandler, 1964), esp. pp. 34-83; Carl G. Hemple, *Aspects of Scientific Explanation* (New York: The Free Press, 1965), chapters 4-6.

5. George Lichtheim, *The Concept of Ideology and Other Essays* (New York: Vintage Books, 1967).

6. A genealogy of this interpretation of the concept of "ideology" would begin with Marx's insights, particularly those contained in *The German Ideology* (London: Lawrence and Wishart, 1970), pp. 46-52, 64-68; and the section on "the fetishism of commodities" in Chapter One of *Capital* (vol. 1; Chicago: Charles H. Kerr, 1906), pp. 81-96. Marx's position has been subsequently developed and extended by such thinkers as: Karl Mannheim, *Ideology and Utopia* (London: Routledge and Kegal Paul, 1936) (hereafter cited as *Utopia*); Henri Lefebrve, *The Sociology of Marx* (New York: Vintage Books, 1969); (hereafter cited as *Marx*); Istvan Meszaros, *Marx's Theory of Alienation* (London: Merlin Press, 1970); George Lukacs, *History and Class Consciousness* (Cambridge, Mass.: MIT Press, 1971). (hereafter cited as *History and Class*)

7. Lefebrve, *Marx*, pp. 69-71.

8. Harold D. Lasswell and Abraham Kaplan, *Power and Society* (New Haven: Yale University Press, 1950), pp. 116-124; Maurice Godelier, "System, Structure and Contradiction in *Das Kapital*," *Introduction to Structuralism*, ed., Michael Lane (New York: Basic Books, 1970), p. 343. (hereafter cited as *Structuralism*)

9. As Roland Barthes has noted with regard to the closely related question of myth: "Myth does not deny things, on the contrary, its function is to talk about them; simply, it purifies them, it makes them innocent, it gives them a natural and eternal justification, it gives them a clarity which is not that of an explanation but that of a statement of fact." See his *Mythologies* (New York: Hill and Wang, 1972), p. 143. In considering ideology, then, as a form of thought which "hides" certain aspects of the social world, we do not mean that these are ignored or excluded; rather, they are transformed and appear as something other than they actually are. In this respect, Barthes refers to myth as "depoliticized speech" which "transforms history into nature."

10. Juergen Habermas, *Toward a Rational Society* (London: Heinemann, 1972); *Communication and the Evolution of Society* (Boston: Beacon, 1979); "On Systematically Distorted Communication," *Inquiry* vol. 13 (Autumn 1970); "Towards a Theory of Communicative Competence," *Inquiry*, vol. 13 (Winter 1970).

11. See also Zygmunt Bauman, *Towards a Critical Sociology* (London: Routledge and Kegan Paul, 1976); Claus Mueller, *The Politics of Communication* (New York: Oxford University Press, 1973).

12. Alvin Gouldner, *The Dialectic of Ideology and Technology* (New York: Seabury, 1976).

13. This distinction is made by Theodore Thass-Thienemann in *Symbolic Behavior* (New York: Washington Square Press, 1968), pp. 17-23. See also,

Ernst Cassirer, *An Essay on Man* (New York: Doubleday, 1944), p. 51 (hereafter cited as *Man*)

14. Philip Wheelwright, *The Burning Fountain* (Bloomington: University of Indiana Press, 1954). p. 19. Wheelwright illustrates the difference between symbol and sign through the example of a cloudy sky. As a natural *sign*, such a sky signals to the perceiver an approaching storm; as a social *symbol*, the same sky would "point beyond itself" and convey the meaning of, say, emotional turmoil or impending disaster. (hereafter cited as *Fountain*)

15. Habermas and Gouldner have demonstrated that there are no "pre-bourgeois" ideologies, inasmuch as the bourgeoisie waged its struggle for ascendancy against an aristocracy rooted in the particularistic tradition of ascriptive status buttressed by sacred authority. Hence, in opposition to those privileged by birth, the bourgeoisie formulated its vision of the good society and its subsequent self-legitimization around appeals to reason, experience, etc. For the first time in human history, therefore, the legitimacy of a ruling class was set out in terms which invited all men to recognize themselves (i.e., through the power of their own reason, rather than through the claims of tradition, sacred authority, and so on) the rightness of the social order inaugurated by the bourgoisie. Concomitantly, however, this social order, based upon *private property*, gave the lie to the generality expressed in ideas. Consequently, ideology has ever been a pretender to reason's throne; the generality of its form is contradicted by the particular, property-based interest which comprises its content. Such contradiction accounts for the usage and effect of an ideology's symbolism—that which takes up where reason has left off. And it is this symbolic content which ideology shares with its forerunner, myth.

Habermas' argument is found in *Legitimation Crisis* (Boston: Beacon, 1975), pp. 20-24; Gouldner's appears in *Ideology and Technology.*

16. Cassirer, *Man* p. 102.

17. Ernest Cassirer, *Language and Myth* (New York: Dover, 1946), p. 10. Wheelwright comments: "Myth . . . is not in the first instance a fiction imposed on one's already given world, but a way of apprehending that world." *Fountain*, p. 159.

With respect to political ideology vis-a-vis political events, Murray Edelman arrives at the same conclusion in *Political Language* (New York: Academic Press, 1977)

18. Claude Levi-Strauss, *Structural Anthropology* (New York: Basic Books, 1963), pp. 200-201; see also Marc Gaboriau, "Structural Anthropology and History," *Structuralism*, pp. 160-161.

19. Ernst Cassirer, *The Myth of the State* (New Haven: Yale University Press, 1946), p. 47.

20. Barthes, *Mythologies*, pp. 127-143.

21. Cassirer, in *Language*, p. 3, states it thusly: "The notion that name and essence bear a necessary and internal relation to each other, that the name does not merely denote but actually *is* the essence of the object, that the

potency of the real thing is contained in the name—that is one of the fundamental assumptions of the mythmaking consciousness itself." (Cassirer's italics)

On the importance of symbolic meaning and context, see also Wheelwright, *Fountain,* pp. 61, 62, 157.

Paul Goodman reminds us of the powerful force which "word magic" exerts in contemporary society; that is, the unity of the word and that to which it refers. He speaks of obscenity as a case in point. Goodman notes that social mores render the mention of certain things as an obscene act; it is obscene to *say* such things, he feels, because the saying of the thing is taken for the thing itself. See his *Speaking and Language* (New York: Random House, 1971), pp. 23, 24.

22. Cassirer (*op. cit., supra,* pp. 56, 57) delineates such a distinction. Since logical-discursive thought relates a concept to data, a concept to another concept and so on, it results in relations which can be manipulated by the mind, making possible the invention of new relations. Conversely, mythical-ideological thought manipulates the mind, as it were; it consists of frozen relations (name—thing) through which thought "is simply captivated by a total impression."

23. Goodman phrases this very cogently: "We judge what works largely according to how we are and what we therefore believe, and how we are largely depends on our language." *Speaking,* p. 26.

24. Stanislaw Ossowski seems to have been referring to the same idea with his term "social consciousness." He defined it as "the ideas that characterize certain milieu . . . the concepts, images, beliefs and evaluations that are more or less common to people of a certain social environment and which are reinforced in the consciousness of particular individuals by mutual suggestion and by the conviction that they are shared by other people in the same group." See *Class Structure in the Social Consciousness* (London: Routledge and Kegan Paul, 1963), p. 6.

25. M. M. Lewis, *Language in Society* (New York: Social Science Publishers, 1948), p. 94.

A short, but thorough, summary of literature related to the idea of "group mind" can be found in Irving L. Janis' *Victims of Groupthink* (Boston: Houghton Mifflin, 1972), pp. 2-13.

26. Joyce A. Hertzler, *A Sociology of Language* (New York: Random House, 1965), esp., pp. 62-66.

27. As Lewis has put it: "Group consciousness is fixed on a range of motive narrower than the full range of actual incentives; so that even in the presence of extending political education, the group, as a group, will remain unaware, or at least uneasily half aware, of the incentives underlying its behavior as a group." *Society,* p. 186.

28. Edelman, *Political Language,* pp. 6-7; see also Wilhelm Reich, *The Mass Psychology of Fascism* (New York: Farrar Straus and Giroux, 1970), esp., Chapter One.

29. Edelman, *Political Language,* p. 28.

30. Lukacs, *History and Class*, pp. 8-12, 48, 49; Mannheim, *Utopia*, pp. 2-4. On the question of "the part and the whole," see Michael Polanyi, *Knowing and Being*, ed., M. Grene (Chicago: The University of Chicago Press, 1969), p. 125.

31. Wheelwright, *Fountain*, pp. 9-11; see also the remarks of William Appleman Williams in *The Roots of the Modern American Empire*, (New York: Random House, 1969), pp. ix-xii.

Theodore W. Adorno describes the historical-critical method in this way: "What dissolves the fetish is the insight that things are not simply so and not otherwise, that they have come to be under certain conditions." Hence, we must look for "the possibility of which their reality has cheated the objects and which is none the less visible in each one." See idem, *Negative Dialectics* (New York: Seabury Press, 1973), pp. 52-54.

32. C. Wright Mills, *The Sociological Imagination* (London: Oxford University Press, 1959), p. 154.

33. Lichtheim, *Other Essays*, Chapter One; Bertell Ollman, *Alienation* (2nd ed.; Cambridge: At the University Press, 1976), pp. 14-64.

34. Juergen Habermas, *Theory and Practice* (London: Heinemann, 1974), p. 12. (hereafter cited as *Theory*.)

35. Habermas, *Theory*, p. 181.

To my knowledge, this principle of critique was first annunciated by Marx in his "Letter to Arnold Ruge," *The Marx-Engels Reader*, ed., Robert C. Tucker (New York: W. W. Norton, 1972), pp. 7-10.

36. Alfred Schutz, "Concept and Theory Formation in the Social Sciences," *The Journal of Philosophy*, vol. 51 (1954).

37. Richard Bernstein, *The Restructuring of Social and Political Theory* (Philadelphia: University of Pennsylvania Press, 1978).

38. Jean Paul Sartre, *Search for a Method* (New York: Vintage Books, 1968), pp. 37, 47, 76-79.

39. Mannheim, *Utopia*, pp. 40-45.

40. On the concept of intentionality, see Stephen Strasser, *Phenomenology and the Human Sciences* (Pittsburgh: Duquesne University Press, 1963), pp. 21-25; Maurice Natanson, *Literature, Philosophy and the Social Sciences* (The Hague: Martinus Nijhoff, 1962), pp. 15-25; idem, *Philosophy of the Social Sciences* (New York: Random House, 1963). H. Spiegelberg, *The Phenomenological Movement* (2nd ed., 2 Vols; The Hague: Martinus Nijhoff, 1971); Alfred Schutz, "Some Leading Concepts in Phenomenology," *Social Research*, vol. 12 (February 1945), pp. 77-97; R. D. Laing, *The Divided Self* (Harmondsworth: Penguin, 1965, pp. 31-38; M. M. Postan, *Fact and Relevance* (Cambridge: At the University Press, 1971), pp. 16-29.

41. Mannheim, *Utopia*, p. 276.

42. *Ibid.*, pp. 276-277.

43. *Ibid.*, pp. 277.

2. Modern Industrialism and the Phenomenon of Bureaucracy

1. Daniel Bell, *The Coming of Post Industrial Society* (New York: Basic Books, 1973).

2. See, for instance, Elisha P. Douglass, *The Coming of Age of American Business* (Chapel Hill: University of North Carolina Press, 1971), pp. 528-531.

3. David Dickson, *Alternative Technology and the Politics of Technical Change* (Glasgow: Fontana/Collins, 1974), pp. 10-95 (hereafter cited as *Alternative Technology)*; Harry Braverman, *Labor and Monopoly Capital* (New York: Monthly Review Press, 1974), pp. 19-20, 193, 230 (hereafter cited as *Labor)*; Frederick J. and Lou Jean Fleron, "Administrative Theory as Repressive Political Theory: The Communist Experience," *Newsletter on Comparative Studies of Communism*, vol. 6 (November 1972); Andre Gorz, "Technical Intelligence and the Capitalist Division of Labor," *Telos* No. 12 (Summer 1972).

4. Dickson *Alternative Technology*, pp. 52, 76.

5. Ray Reece, *The Sun Betrayed* (Boston: South End Press, 1979), pp. 89-93.

6. A study which documents this subject with particular attention to the engineering profession in the US is David Noble's *America by Design* (New York: Alfred A. Knopf, 1977).

7. Nicos Poulantzas, *Political Power and Social Classes* (London: NLB, 1973) (hereafter cited as *Power and Classes)*; Erik Olin Wright, *Class, Crisis and the State* (London: NLB, 1978). (hereafter cited as *Class)*

8. Wright *Class*, pp. 15-16.

9. Irwin Yellowitz, *Industrialization and the American Labor Movement, 1850-1900*, (Port Washington, N.Y.: Kennikat, 1977).

For a brief treatment of the same phenomenon, see Irving Louis Horowitz, *Ideology and Utopia in the United States: 1956-1976* (New York: Oxford University Press, 1977), pp. 109-111.

10. Alvin W. Gouldner, *Patterns of Industrial Bureaucracy* (New York: Free Press, 1954) (hereafter cited as *Patterns)*; William A. Faunce, *Problems of an Industrial Society* (New York: McGraw Hill, 1968); Georges Friedmann, *The Anatomy of Work* (New York: The Free Press of Glencoe, 1961).

11. Richard Edwards, *Contested Terrain* (New York: Basic Books, 1979).

12. Raymond Aron, *18 Lectures on Industrial Society* (London: Weidenfeld and Nicolson, 1967), pp. 73-74.

13. Gerth and Mills, *Weber*, pp. 196-198, 205-209.

14. Braverman, *Labor*.

15. It is interesting to note that Frederick W. Taylor, the founder of "scientific management," understood his efforts in just this way; namely, replacing the organization of the workplace by workmen with an organization of the workplace of the workmen and of all operations by management. See *The Principles of Scientific Management* (New York: Harper, 1911), esp. p. 36. H. S. Person, a former Managing Director of the Taylor Society, saw the

problem which Taylor attacked thusly: "mechanization of industry was well underway, operations were becoming specialized, workers at machines were more scattered and more difficult to supervise, and planning, supervision and coordination had not developed with specialization." These remarks appear in *Scientific Management in American Industry*, ed., H. S. Person (New York: Harper, 1929.) p. 2.

16. *Capital*, (Chicago: Charles H. Kerr, 1906), vol. 1, chapter one, section 2; chapter six and *passim*.

17. Marx discerned this tendency as early as 1849 in "Wage Labor and Capital," *Karl Marx and Frederick Engles: Selected Works* (Moscow: Progress Publishers, 1968), pp. 64-94. The rudiments of these ideas can also be found in "Manifesto of the Communist Party," pp. 35-63; esp. pp. 41, 42.

18. *Op. cit.*, p. 233 and *passim*.

19. Frederick J. Fleron, Jr., *Technology and Communist Culture* (New York: Praeger, 1977), pp. 1-67.

20. Raymond Aron, *The Industrial Society* (New York: Praeger, 1967), esp. pp. 101, 117, 118.

21. Claude Lefort, "What Is Bureaucracy?", *Telos* No. 22 (Winter 1974-75).

22. Adam Przeworski, "Proletariat into a Class: The Process of Class Formation from Karl Kautsky's *The Class Struggle* to Present Controversies," *Politics and Society*, vol. 7 (No. 4, 1977).

23. Another thinker who has devoted considerable attention to the social side of bureaucracy is Michel Crozier. See his *The Bureaucratic Phenomenon* (Chicago: The University of Chicago Press, 1964); and idem, *The Stalled Society* (New York: Viking, 1973).

24. Gouldner, *Patterns*; Richard Balzer, *Clockwork* (Garden City, N.Y.: Doubleday, 1976.)

25. V. Klimov, "Arsenal Rukovoditelya," *Sovety deputatov trudyashchikhsya* (July 1977).

26. I refer, here, to the rationalist school of philosophy, culminating in Hegel, which postulates the sovereignty of reason as the constructor of the world. In coming to know this world, reason "returns to itself," that is, it comes to know the world and itself as one.

27. Herbert Marcuse, for instance, called attention to such things as the "rational" (in the modern sense) construction of kill and overkill ratios in defense planning. He argued that the effects of such rationality, Strangelovian doomsday machines, are manifestly irrational and, therefore, could only have resulted from an inadequate, one-sided or, perhaps, perverted usage of "rationality." See his *Negations* (Boston: Beacon Press, 1968), p. 208.

I would submit that it is precisely because of the connotations of the term—the sovereignty of reason, the idea of thought guiding action, the alternatives as "irrational"—that the absurdity of doomsday machines presents itself as rational (and, therefore, good, proper and the like) behavior.

28. Max Weber, *The Theory of Social and Economic Organizations* (New York: The Free Press, 1947), p. 115. (hereafter cited as *Economic Organizations*)

29. *Ibid.*, p. 117.

30. *Ibid.*

31. For discussions of modern rationality as a means-oriented viewpoint, see: Aron, *The Industrial Society, op. cit.*, pp. 67-72, 102, 103; Habermas, *Theory and Practice* (London: Heinemann, 1974), esp., pp. 41-81, 263-282; and idem, *Toward A Rational Society* (London: Heinemann, 1971), pp. 50-122; Max Horkheimer, *Eclipse of Reason* (New York: Oxford Univ. Press, 1947), pp. 3-20; and, idem, *Critical Theory* (New York: Herder and Herder, 1972), pp. 178-181; Laurence H. Tribe, "Technology Assessment and the Fourth Discontinuity: The Limits of Instrumental Rationality," *Southern California Law Review*, vol. 46 (June 1973).

32. C. Wright Mills, *The Sociological Imagination* (New York: Oxford University Press), p. 170.

33. Ernst Cassirer points out that the pursuit of scientific knowledge was in many respects tied to myth and magic as late as the early part of the eighteenth century. See *The Myth of the State* (New Haven: Yale University Press, 1946), p. 294.

34. The best single study of this is William Leiss' *The Domination of Nature* (New York: George Braziller, 1972). Leiss has also dealt with the treatment which this problem—the progressive dominance of scientific rationality as a mode of thought and the attendant dominance of man over nature—has received at the hands of the Frankfurt School in "The Problem of Man and Nature in the Work of the Frankfurt School," *Philosophy of the Social Sciences*, no. 5 (1975).

See also, on this subject, Herbert Marcuse's *One-Dimensional Man* (Boston: Beacon Press, 1964), esp. chapter six; Horkheimer's *Eclipse of Reason*, chapter three.

35. Aron, *supra*, feels that "the application of the scientific spirit to the organization of production is the essence of an industrial society." (pp. 59-60)

36. *Ibid.*, p. 61.

37. Leiss, *The Domination of Nature*.

38. It should be clear to the reader here that I am treating "science" in this context as a pure type.

39. Leiss, *supra*, p. 199.

40. Gerth and Mills, *Weber*, pp. 212-216.

41. D. K. Hart and W. G. Scott refer to this technical-rational conception as "the organizational imperative," an idea based on two presuppositions: (1) *"Whatever is good for man can only be achieved through modern organization;* (2) *Therefore, all behavior must enhance the health of such modern organizations."* See their "The Organizational Imperative," *Administration and Society*, vol. 7 (November 1975). (Hart and Scott's italics.)

42. Habermas, *Toward a Rational Society*, p. 82.

43. *Ibid.*, p. 83. (Italics added.)

44. *Ibid.*, p. 59.

45. Herbert Marcuse has remarked: "In this universe, technology also provides the great rationalization of the unfreedom of man and demonstrates the 'technical' impossibility of being autonomous, or determining one's own life. For this unfreedom appears neither as irrational nor as political, but rather as submission to the technical apparatus which enlarges the comforts of life and increases the productivity of labor. Technological rationality thus protects rather than cancels the legitimacy of domination and the instrumentalist horizon opens on a rationally totalitarian society." See *One-Dimensional Man*, pp. 158-159.

46. See, in particular, Habermas, *Theory and Practice*, p. 255.

47. Juergen Habermas, *Legitimation Crisis* (Boston: Beacon, 1975), esp. p. 47; and, by the same author, *Communication and the Evolution of Society* (Boston: Beacon, 1979), chapter five.

48. Cassirer, *op. cit.*, pp. 281-289.

49. Joyce A. Hertzler, *A Sociology of Language* (New York: Random House, 1965), p. 334.

50. *Ibid.*, p. 341.

51. Juergen Habermas, *Knowledge and Human Interests* (Boston: Beacon, 1972).

52. Lenin, for example, promoted the adoption of the Taylor system of "scientific management" from the very beginning of the Soviet order. See *Selected Works* (New York: International Publishers, 1943), pp. 332-333.

A more recent illustration of Soviet borrowing from American experience would be the gigantic Kama truck plant, the managerial structure of which was modelled directly on that of the American "big three" auto producers. See my "Theory and Ideology in Soviet Administration: A Rejoinder to Vidmer," *Administration and Society*, vol. 12 (May 1980).

53. Charles E. Lindblom, *Politics and Markets* (New York: Basic Books, 1978).

54. Alvin W. Gouldner, *The Dialectic of Ideology and Technology* (New York: Seabury, 1976); Goeran Therborn, *What Does the Ruling Class Do When It Rules?* (London: NLB, 1978) (hereafter cited as *Ruling Class*); Langdon Winner, *Autonomous Technology* (Boston: M.I.T. Press, 1976), p. 41.

55. Harold D. Lasswell and Abraham Kaplan, *Power and Society*, (New Haven: Yale University Press, 1950), esp., p. 128.

56. Therborn, *Ruling Class*; C. Wright Mills, *The Power Elite* (New York: Oxford University Press, 1956); Kenneth Prewitt and Alan Stone, *The Ruling Elites* (New York: Harper and Row, 1973); Maurice Zeitlin, "Corporate Ownership and Control: The Large Corporation and the Capitalist Class," *American Journal of Sociology*, vol. 79 (March 1974); P. Sargant Florence, *The Logic of British and American Industry* (Chapel Hill: University of North Carolina Press, 1953), pp. 176-208. (hereafter cited as *Industry*)

On the Soviet side, see Vladimir Anderle, *Managerial Power in the Soviet Union* (Westmead, U.K.: Saxon House, 1976); Stephen White "Contradiction and Change in State Socialism," *Soviet Studies*, vol. 27 (October 1975).

57. Florence, *Industry*, Douglass, *op. cit*; Graham Bannock, *The Jugger-nauts* (New York: Bobbs-Merrill, 1971); Richard Parker, *The Myth of the Middle Class* (New York: Harper and Row, 1972); Michael Best and William Connolly, *The Politicized Economy* (Lexington, Mass.: D.C. Heath, 1976).

58. Robert L. Heilbronner, *Business Civilization in Decline* (New York: W. W. Norton, 1976); Authur Selwyn Miller, *The Modern Corporate State* (West-port, Conn.: Greenwood Press, 1976); Francis E. Rourke, *Bureaucracy, Poli-tics and Public Policy* (2nd ed.; Boston: Little Brown, 1976); Claus Offe, "Political Authority and Class Structure—An Analysis of Late Capitalist Societies," *International Journal of Sociology;* vol. 2 (Spring 1972); and, idem, "Further Comments on Mueller and Neusuess," *Telos*, No. 25 (Fall 1975); and, with Volker Ronge, "Theses on the Theory of the State," *New German Critique*, No. 6 (Fall 1975).

59. Paul Baran and Paul Sweezy, *Monopoly Capital* (New York: Monthly Review Press, 1968).

60. Offe, *International Journal of Sociology* (Spring 1972); James O'Connor, *The Fiscal Crisis of the State* (New York; St. Martin's Press, 1973); Habermas, *Legitimation Crisis.*

61. James Burnham, *The Managerial Revolution* (Harmondsworth: Pen-guin, 1945).

62. John Kenneth Galbraith, *The New Industrial State* (New York: The American Library, 1967).

63. *Inter alia*, Zbigniew K. Brzezinski, *Ideology and Power in Soviet Politics* (2nd ed.; New York: Frederick A. Praeger, 1967); and, with Samuel P. Huntington, *Political Power: USA/USSR* (New York: Viking, 1964); Leon Trotsky, *The Revolution Betrayed* (London: New Park, 1973); Tony Cliff, *State Capitalism in Russia* (London: Pluto Press, 1974).

64. Antonio Carlo, "The Socio-Economic Nature of the USSR," *Telos*, No. 21 (Fall 1974). and, idem, "Structural causes of the Soviet coexistence policy," *Soviet Foreign Policy: Its Social and Economic Conditions*, ed. by Egbert Jahn (London: Allison and Busby, 1978).

65. Hillel H. Ticktin's work includes: "Towards a Political Economy of the USSR," *Critique*, No. 1 (1973); "Soviet Society and Professor Bettelheim," *Critique*, No. 6 (1976); "Class Structure and the Soviet Elite," *Critique*, No. 9 (1978); and "The relationship between detente and Soviet economic re-forms," in Jahn, *op. cit.*, pp. 41-56.

66. Rainer Paris, "Class Structure and Legitimatory Public Sphere," *New German Critique*, No. 6 (Spring 1975).

67. Anderle, *Managerial Power;* White, *Soviet Studies.*

68. Alfred D. Chander, Jr., *Strategy and Structure* (Garden City, N.Y.: Anchor Books, 1966).

69. See, on this subject, Noble *op. cit.*, pp. 69-83.

70. Gouldner, *Patterns.*

71. Reinhard Bendix, *Work and Authority in Industry* (New York: Wiley, 1956); H. Benyon and R. M. Blackburn, *Perceptions of Work* (Cambridge: At the University Press, 1972).

72. Balzer, *op.cit.*

73. See the articles by Fleron, cited in notes 3 and 19 of this chapter.

74. By March/April of 1918, Lenin was already advocating all the essentials of the industrial order common to capitalism—hierarchical subordination, labor discipline, strict accounting and control. The following passage shows, perhaps, the identity which he saw between socialism and industrialism given a change in property relations: "Introduce accurate and conscientious accounting of money, manage economically, do not be lazy, do not steal, observe the strictest discipline during work—it is precisely such slogans which were justly scorned by the revolutionary proletariat when the bourgeoisie concealed its rule as an exploiting class by the commandments that now, after the overthrow of the bourgeoisie, are becoming the immediate and principal slogans of the moment. The practical application of these slogans by the *Soviet* government, by the methods that it employs, on the basis of *its* laws, is the necessary and *sufficient* condition for the final victory of socialism." *Selected Works*, pp. 313-350; esp. 318, 319 (Lenin's italics)

Somewhat earlier (December 1917), Lenin was calling for what might be thought to be the antithesis of socialist cooperative ethics, i.e., organized mass competition. Again, it was the interests of industrial production, which competition was seen to further, which seemed uppermost in his mind. See his "Kak organizovat' sorevnovanie?" (Moscow: Politicheskaya literatura, 1969).

75. Quoted in D. Gvishiani, *Organization and Management* (Moscow: Progress, 1972), p. 57. (Gvishiani's italics)

76. Chris Goodey, "Factory Committees and the Dictatorship of the Proletariat," *Critique*, No. 3, (1974); Carmen J. Siranni, "Workers' Control in the Era of World War 1: A Comparative Analysis of European Experience" *Theory and Society*, vol. 9, (January 9, 1980).

77. Lenin, *Selected Works*, p. 342. It is interesting to note that Soviet writers on the subject of management in a socialist soviety quote this passage with approbation. See, for instance, D. Gvishiani, *Organization and Management*, p. 92; also F. B. Sadykov, "O vzaimootnosheniyakh rukovodietelei i mass," *Nauchnoe upravlenie obshchestvom*, ed., V. G. Afanas'ev (Moscow: Misl', 1967), p. 60.

78. For the US, see the works cited in notes 54, 56 and 58 of this chapter. On the Soviet experience the literature is voluminous. I have summed up and subjected to criticism some of it in my "Information and Participation in Soviet Local Government," *The Journal of Politics* (forthcoming).

79. *The End of Liberalism* (New York: Norton, 1969), pp. 19-27. (Lowi's italics)

80. Offe, *International Journal of Sociology*, (Spring 1972).

81. *Ibid.*

82. On the idea of "focal institution" which interpenetrates and coordinates a plurality of organizations in society, see William H. Friedland, "A Sociological Approach to Modernization," *Modernization by Design*, ed.,

Chandler Morse, *et al* (Ithaca: Cornell University Press, 1968), esp. p. 58: Arthur Stinchcombe, "Social Structure and Organizations," in *Handbook of Organizations*, ed., James G. March (Chicago: Rand McNally, 1965), p. 189.

83. *Op. cit.*, p. 88.

84. *Ibid.*, pp. 88-89; See also Randall Bartlett's, *The Economic Foundations of Political Power* (New York: Free Press, 1973).

85. This seems to be precisely what Lowi (*op. cit.*, p. 88) has in mind when he remarks: "The more clear and legitimized the representation of a group or its leader in policy formation, the less voluntary is membership in that group and the more necessary is loyalty to its leadership for people who share the interests in question."

86. Raymond Aron sums up the problem of citizenship in modern industrial society by noting that "the modern state is first of all an administrative state. Citizens, as economic subjects, are permanently subjected to the rules of officials who fix the laws of competition between the individuals and determine the consequences of the laws in each circumstance. This administrative power is in a sense 'depersonalized' and sometimes deprived of its political character: officials command in the capacity of officials and citizens obey the laws and the anonymous representatives of the State." See "Social Class, Political Class, Ruling Class," *Class, Status and Power*, eds., R. Bendix and S. M. Lipset (2nd ed.; New York: The Free Press, 1968), p. 205.

87. In recent years, again following to some extent the American experience, the Soviets have developed a considerable interest in the phenomenon of "public opinion." See, in particular, R. A. Safarov, *Obshchestvennoe mnenie i gosudarstvennoe upravlenie* (Moscow: Yuridicheskaya literatura, 1975).

88. Henry Jacoby, *The Bureaucratization of the World* (Berkeley: University of California Press, 1973), pp. 154-155.

3. Contradictions in Administrative Rationality

1. A short list of American authors in whose writings these thoughts appear would include: Frederick W. Taylor, *The Principles of Scientific Management* (New York: Harper, 1911); Luther Gulick and L. Urwick, eds., *Papers on the Science of Administration* (New York: Columbia University, Institute of Public Administration, 1937); A. E. Buck, *Administrative Consolidation in State Government* (5th ed.; New York: National Municipal League, 1930); James G. March and Herbert Simon, *Organizations* (New York: John Wiley and Sons, 1965); George S. Counts, "The Impact of Technological Change," *The Planning of Change*, ed., Warren G. Bennis *et al* (New York: Holt, Rinehart and Winston, 1961), pp. 20-28. Interestingly enough, Daniel Bell, who forecasts *The Coming of Post-Industrial Society* (New York: Basic Books, 1973), sees science and technology as precisely such an autonomous and independent force propelling change in society (esp. pp. 188-195).

To be sure, there is a large body of writing on the American side which scarcely addresses itself to such matters—the "human relations" school, or that of "organizational development," for example. These approaches, far from diverging from the characterization which I have presented, in fact presuppose it and concern themselves with the lag between the *desideratum* of rationality and actual human behavior.

Some Soviet authors who take up this theme of rationality are: V. V. Poshataev, "Rol'i mesto nauchno-tekhnicheskoi revolyutsii v kommunisti-cheskom stroitel'stve," *Problemy nauchnogo kommunizma*, ed., V. G. Afanas'ev (vol. 7; Moscow: Mysl', 1973), pp. 6-30; V. A. Karpushin *et al*, eds., *Nauchnyi kommunizm* (Moscow: Politicheskaya literatura, 1965), pp. 209-229; P. A. Rachkov, *Rol' nauki v stroitel'stvo kommunizma* (Moscow: Moscow University, 1969), pp. 4-140; G. A. Prudenskii, *Vremya i trud* (Moscow: Misl', 1964), esp., pp. 145-157.

2. Variations on this theme can be found in Chester I. Barnard, *The Functions of the Executive* (Cambridge: Harvard University Press, 1958); pp. 4, 22-37; Herbert A. Simon, *Administrative Behavior* (2nd ed.; New York: Macmillan, 1960); Bertram M. Gross, *The Managing of Organizations* (vol. l; New York: The Free Press of Glencoe, 1964), p. 34; Anthony Downs, *Inside Bureaucracy* (Boston: Little Brown, 1967), pp. 32, 33, 54-56.

Soviet examples of same would include V. P. Korienko, *Obshchestvennoe razdelenie truda v period perekhoda k kommunizmu* (Moscow: Ekonomicheskaya literatura, 1963), p. 33; G. E. Glezerman, "Vvedenie," in his *Stroitel'stvo kommuniza i razvitie obshchestvennykh otnoshenii* (Moscow: Nauka, 1966), p. 12.

3. Writers such as William J. Gore express this in almost transcendental terms. New management techniques, he writes, "represent a coming to fruition of the glorious anticipations of Frederick Taylor and those others who conceived a true science of management seventy years ago. But whereas Scientific Management could not find the technology to fulfill this promise, Management Science has arrived just as a wave of technological development is bursting over us. There is no need to describe what inte-grating bands of computers, statistical decision theory and linear program-ming have come to mean in the few short years they have been available. . . . So wonderous is the paraphernalia of modern management that the layman may feel that it revolves according to complicated and mysterious laws beyond the ken of the uninitiated." The "initiated," however, realize that all depends on a "rational system of action . . . the formally sanc-tioned, politically legitimized basis for mobilizing a society's talent and resources behind its manifest purposes." Gore goes on to claim that "even the masses (presumedly, the "uninitiated") understand its essential dy-namics and honor its central place in their affairs." See his *Administrative Decision-Making* (New York: John Wiley and Sons, 1964), pp. 3, 4.

4. Amatai Etzioni, *Modern Organizations* (Englewood Cliffs: Prentice Hall, 1964) p. 1. Etzioni (p. 3) also believes that *"organizational rationality and human happiness go hand and hand."* (Etzioni's italics).

5. Peter F. Drucker, *The New Society* (New York: Harper and Brothers, 1950), p. 6, (Drucker's italics).

6. Simon, *Administrative Behavior*, p. xxiv (Simon's italics); see also March and Simon, *Organizations*, p. 141.

William Leiss has critiqued this perspective as follows: "Through a curious process of inversion the means (technological innovations) come to govern the ends (values and norms): men have become the 'objects' rather than the 'subjects' of their own activity. It is not that men are experiencing an essentially novel phase of social development, for most men have passed through the historical record as the objects of forces which they neither comprehended nor controlled; the paradox is that this persistent phenomenon should be *revalued* and now be regarded as bursting with 'the promise of new freedom.' The element of passivity in these conceptions . . . is the unintended admission of the truth that most men remain the objects of their practice, i.e., that their productive activity somehow results in new circumstances to which perforce they must adapt themselves. This passivity is clearly expressed in the notion that men must 'learn how to take full advantage of the humane potentialities of technological progress,' a formula which implies an adaptive mode of behavior and which confuses means and ends." See his "The Social Consequences of Technical Progress," *Canadian Public Administration*, vol. 13 (Fall 1970); esp., p. 255. (Leiss' italics).

7. Philip Selznick, *Leadership in Administration* (New York: Harper and Row, 1957), pp. 14, 15.

8. Gross, *The Managing of Organizations*, pp. 370-373.

9. Simon is quite candid on this point. "Knowledge of administration is amoral . . . for it is knowledge of how to manipulate other human beings." *Public Administration* (New York: Alfred A. Knopf, 1958), p. 22. Warren G. Bennis refers to such as the core of the administrator's "leadership" role: "control over rewards, an agent who manipulates these rewards and an influence process. Power residing in an agent leads to influence. This influence is viewed as a consequent variable dependent on the ability of the agent to manipulate the approved rewards." See his "Leadership Theory and Administrative Behavior," Bennis *et al, The Planning of Change*, pp. 434-445; esp., p. 441. Barnard likewise finds the "essence of the executive functions" in "deliberate, conscious and specialized control" of those factors which are seen to influence the behavior of any subordinate (e.g., "purposes, desires, impulses," or any external alternatives which he might recognize). *The Functions of the Executive*, p. 17, 96-113.

For examples of Soviet writings on the use of incentives to secure conformity between the goals of the plan and the behavior of the enterprise, and between the goals of the enterprise and the behavior of its members, see B. Sukharevskii, "Sotsialisticheskoe predpriyatie i narodnoe khozyaistov," *Voprosy ekonomiki*, No. 5 (May 1963); N. Garetovskii, "Finansovoe planirovanie i sistema finansovykh planov v narodnom khozyaistve," *Finansy SSSR*, No. 5 (May 1967).

10. Etzioni chooses "compliance" as the basic factor in modern organiza-

tions. "Compliance is the relationship consisting of the power employed by superiors to control subordinates and the orientation of the subordinates to this power." *Complex Organizations* (New York: The Free Press, 1961), p. xv.

11. Herbert Marcuse, *Soviet Marxism* (New York: Vintage Books, 1961), pp. 64-76. This writer has come across no Soviet writings which would conflict with Marcuse's characterization, and a good number which would confirm it; e.g., G. E. Glezerman, "Perekhod ot sotsializma k kommunizmu i stiranie klassovykh granei," in Glezerman, *op. cit.*, pp. 17-54; esp., pp. 41, 42; L. N. Kogan and V. I. Loktev, "Sociological aspects of the modelling of towns," *Town, Country and People*, ed., G. V. Osipov (London: Tavistock, 1969); M. K. Popov, "Nekotorye problemy sotsial'nogo razvitiya goroda," Afanas'ev, *op cit.*, pp. 98-127.

12. As George Lichtheim has pointed out, history, from a Marxian point of view, can only be subject to "laws" insofar as it is not consciously made by men. To speak simultaneously of socialism (an epoch in which men for the first time consciously make history) and "objective laws," which govern socialist society, is patently absurd. Soviet writers, nonetheless, do just this. Rudi Supek, in commenting on this same phenomenon, has surmised that "objective laws" are a device used by the leadership to legitimize its broad-range policies and are, therefore, the more evident and the more important in official Soviet pronouncements in those cases in which the leadership's goals and interests cannot be readily made to square with empirical reality. Moreover, he notes that "the transformation of political voluntarism into 'objective laws of social development' also transformed sociological positivism back into social apologetics, and deprived [Soviet] Marxism of both dialectics and the capacity for critical thinking." See his "Sociology and Marxism," *International Journal of Sociology*, vol. 1 (Spring 1971); Lichtheim's point is made in *The Concept of Ideology* (New York: Vintage Books, 1967), p. 21.

13. The nearest thing to a list of these laws which I have seen appears in M. A. Suslov's *Na putyakh stroitel'stva kommunizma* (vol. 2; Moscow: Politizdat, 1977), pp. 115-120.

For a critique of this conception of "objecive laws" under socialism, see my review of his book in *Critique*, No. 13 (Spring 1981).

14. V. G. Afanas'ev, "O soderzhanii (osnovykh funktsiyakh) upravleniya sotsialisticheskim obshchestvom" in his *Nauchnoe upravlenie obshchestvom* (Moscow: Misl', 1967), pp. 5-7.

15. Rachkov, *Rol' nauki v stroitel'stvo Kommunizma, op. cit.*, pp. 141, 142.

16. Karpushin, *Nauchnyi Kommunizm*, p. 5 (emphasis in original). Karpushin discusses "scientific communism" and its "objective laws" on pp. 5-10, 51-52.

17. "Interesy i upravlenie obshchestvennymi protsessami" in Afanas'ev, *op. cit., supra*, pp. 174-175; see also V. G. Afanas'ev *Nauchnyi kommunizm* (2nd ed.; Moscow: Politizdat, 1969), p. 211; B. A. Gryaznov, *et al, Organizatsionnopartiinaya rabota: problemy i opyt* (Moscow: Moskovskii rabochii, 1974), p. 3.

18. Yu. A. Tikhomirov, "Sovetskii apparat i ego kadry" in his *Sluzhashchii*

sovetskogo gosudarstvennogo apparata (Moscow: Yuridicheskaya literatura, 1970), p. 5.

19. B. D. Lebin and M. N. Perfil'ev, *Kadry apparata upravleniya v SSSR* (Leningrad: Nauka, 1970), p. 15.

20. Afanas'ev, *Nauchnoe upravlenie obshchestvom*, pp. 5, 6.

21. This raises the issue of "creative administration" which we shall meet below.

22. D. Gvishiani, *Organization and Management* (Moscow: Progress Publishers, 1972), p. 111.

23. This argument is made by Alvin Gouldner, *The Coming Crisis of Western Sociology* (New York: Basic Books, 1970), pp. 50-56; Jurgen Habermas, *Knowledge and Human Interests* (Boston: Beacon Press, 1972), pp. 4, 176-198, 311-319.

24. For examples of this desideratum, see the essay by William O. Stanley, "The Collapse of Automatic Adjustment" in Bennis *et al*, *The Planning of Change*, pp. 28-34; and, *ibid.*, Ernest Greenwood's "The Practice of Science and the Science of Practice," pp. 73-82.

25. This approaches the status of an article of faith in the administrative literature known to me. It is treated by *inter alia*, the following American authors: Taylor, *The Principles of Scientific Management;* Gulick and Urwick, *Papers on the Science of Administration*, March and Simon, esp. pp. 62-81, 158; Simon, *Administrative Behavior*, pp. 110, 111; Simon *et al*, p. 493; Barnard, *The Functions of the Executive, passim;* Gore, *Administrative Decision-Making*, pp. 3-14. Among Soviet authors, we find references to same in O. V. Kozlova, *Tekhnika, tekhnologiya i kadry upravleniya proizvodstvom* (Moscow: Ekonomika, 1973), pp. 33, 34; A. M. Omarov, *Nauchnye osnovy upravleniya sotsialisticheskoi ekonomikoi* (Moscow: Misl', 1973), pp. 44, 45; M. K. Popov, *op. cit.*, pp. 110, 111; G. V. Barabashev, *Raionnyi, gorodskoi sovet na sovremennom etate* (Moscow: Yuridisheskaya literatura, 1975), p. 100; T. Kiselev, "Nauchnyi podkhod," *Sovety deputatov trudyashchikhsya* (January 1977), pp. 8-17.

26. C. Wright Mills puts it thusly: "The detailed division of labor means, of course, that the individual does not carry through the whole process of work to its final product; but it also means that under many modern conditions the process itself is invisible to him. The product as the goals of his work is legally and psychologically detached from him, and this detachment cuts the nerve of meaning which work might otherwise gain from its technical process. [Hence] . . . the chance to develop and use individual rationality is often destroyed by the centralization of decision and the formal rationality which bureaucracy entails. The expropriation which modern work organization has carried through thus goes far beyond the expropriation of ownership; rationality itself has been expropriated from work and any total view and understanding of its process." See his *White Collar* (New York: Oxford University Press, 1951), pp. 225, 226.

27. Robert Blauner's *Alienation and Freedom* (Chicago: The University of Chicago Press, 1964), is an example of this notion of alienation in the

American literature. I am unaware of any serious Soviet attempts to deal with this concept as it might apply to the Soviet Union (presumedly, since the USSR is "socialist," alienation, *ex definitio,* does not exist). We take up solutions to the effects of alienation which have been advanced in the professional literature on administration in each country in Chapter 5.

28. Robin Blackburn outlines the manner in which critical concepts, such as alienation, have been emasculated in modern social science in "A Brief Guide to Bourgeois Ideology," *The Capitalist System,* ed., Richard C. Edwards *et al* (Englewood Cliffs: Prentice Hall, 1972), pp. 36-45.

29. A thorough treatment of this "objective" side of the concept of alienation can be found in Istvan Meszaros, *Marx's Theory of Alienation* (London: Merlin Press, 1964); Bertell Ollman, *Alienation* (2nd ed.; Cambridge: At the University Press, 1976); Trent Schroyer, *The Critique of Domination* (New York: George Braziller, 1973), p. 75-100.

30. Studies which have analyzed the basic structure of factory production from the perspective of alienation include: H. Benyon and R. M. Blackburn, *Perceptions of Work* (Cambridge: Cambridge University Press, 1972); William A. Faunce, *Problems of an Industrial Society* (New York: Mc-Graw Hill, 1968); and *idem,* "Automation in the Automobile Industry: Some Consequences for In-Plant Structure," *American Sociological Review,* vol. 23 (August 1958).

31. P. Sargant Florence links the subjective aspect of motivation to the objective features of modern organization. The "incentive to work," he writes, "is checked at the outset as soon as he [the worker] finds himself divided off as a mere employee, from the ownership of the products of his labour." See *The Logic of British and American Industry* (Chapel Hill: University of North Carolina Press, 1953), pp. 273-275.

32. A representative definition of organizational efficiency comes from Herbert A. Simon who refers to it as: "the achieving of *the greatest possible results with given opportunity costs* or the achieving of *a given level of results with the lowest possible opportunity costs."* See his *Public Administration,* p. 493. (Simon's italics.) See also March and Simon, *Organizations,* pp. 62, 78-81, 158; Timothy Costello, "The Change Process in Municipal Government," *Emerging Patterns in Urban Administration,* ed., G. F. Brown and T. P. Murphy (Lexington, Mass.: D. C. Heath, 1970), pp. 13-32.

33. This can be illustrated by means of a simple example. Suppose the productivity of a worker (another name for his "efficiency") rises from X to $4X$ while the cost to the organization represented by his wages rises from Y to $2Y$. In this case, the organization has doubled its efficiency (product:cost). On the other hand, the worker *qua* individual has seen his efficiency cut in half; he now produces four times the product for only twice the remuneration.

34. Reinhard Bendix, "Bureaucracy: The Problem and Its Setting," *American Sociological Review,* vol. 12 (October 1947).

35. Alvin W. Gouldner, *The Dialectic of Ideology and Technology* (New York: Seabury, 1976), pp. 242-243.

4. Ideologies of Administrative Leadership: The Mantle of Science

1. For an example of this approach, see F. X. Sutton, *et al*, *The American Business Creed* (Cambridge, Mass: Harvard University Press, 1956).
2. Reinhard Bendix, *Work and Authority in Industry* (New York: Wiley, 1956). (hereafter cited as *Work and Authority*)
3. Theodore Nichols, *Ownership, Control and Ideology* (London: George Allen and Unwin, 1969), p. 212.
4. The discussion of alienation in the previous chapter might predict and at least partially explain this situation. Without recourse to the concept of alienation, however, a number of scholars have documented this phenomenon. See, for instance, Bendix, *Work and Authority*, and, idem, "Bureaucracy: The Problem and Its Setting," *American Sociological Review*, vol. 12 (October 1947), pp. 502-507; Alvin W. Gouldner, *Patterns*, chapter 7; Peter M. Blau and W. Richard Scott, *Formal Organizations* (San Francisco: Chandler, 1962), esp., pp. 140-141; Michel Crozier, *The Stalled Society* (New York: Viking Press, 1973) pp. 30-32, 58.
5. Deena Weinstein devotes considerable attention to this subject in *Bureaucratic Opposition* (New York: Pergamon Press, 1979) See also, Michel Crozier, *The Bureaucratic Phenomenon* (Chicago: The University of Chicago Press, 1964), esp. p. 55; and Peter M. Blau, *The Dynamics of Bureaucracy* (2nd ed.; Chicago: The University of Chicago Press, 1963), esp., pp. 232-233.
6. Two studies which document such for the U.S. Federal Government are: Robert Vaughn, *The Spoiled System* Washington, D.C.: Public Interest Research Group, 1972); and Jay M. Shafritz, *Public Personnel Management* (New York: Praeger, 1975).
7. J. Allan Winter, "Elective Affinities between Religious Beliefs and Ideologies of Management in Two Eras," *American Journal of Sociology*, vol. 79 (March 1974)
8. James G. March and Herbert A. Simon, *Organizations* (New York: John Wiley and Sons, 1965), p. 78. March and Simon go on to list a few methods which might be useful in securing this desideratum without undermining the position of the superior (pp. 78-81). One of these involves social relations and family pressure, whereby the wives of subordinates are invited to social gatherings by the wives of executives in the hope that the former will acquire the value system of the latter and transmit it to their husbands. March and Simon do, however, note that such practices raise "questions of ethical desirability."
9. Frederick W. Taylor, *Principles of Scientific Management*, (New York: Harper and Brothers, 1911). (hereafter cited as *Scientific Management*)
10. For more recent examples of Taylorism's influence on American administrative thinking, see H. R. Nissley, "Rules of Work Simplification for Supervisors," *Management Review*, vol. 53 (January 1954), and Peter Chambers, "Frederick Winslow Taylor: A Much-Maligned Management Pioneer," *Management Review*, vol. 62 (February 1973).
11. Victor A. Thompson, *Bureaucracy and the Modern World* (Morristown, N.J.: General Learning Press, 1976), p. 122.

12. Taylor, *Scientific Management*, p. 119.

13. Charles R. Milton, *Ethics and Expediency in Personnel Management* (Columbia: University of South Carolina Press, 1970), pp. 63-77.

14. For a discussion of psychological testing and industrial psychology in this vein, see Loren Baritz, *The Servants of Power* (Middletown, Conn.: Wesleyan University Press, 1960).

15. Taylor, *Scientific Management*, p. 34.

16. H. S. Person, *Scientific Management in American Industry* (New York: Harper, 1929), p. 17.

17. Allyn Morrow and Frederick Thayer, "Materialism and Humanism: Organization Theory's Odd Couple" *Administration and Society*, vol. 10 (May 1978).

18. David Noble, *America by Design* (New York: Alfred A. Knopf, 1977).

19. As Harry Braverman has pointed out, the success of the Taylor system in this regard is reflected in the fact that it is no longer an identifiable proselytizing sect. That is, "its fundamental teachings," in Braverman's words, "have become the bedrock of all work design," thus obviating the need for continued propaganda on their behalf. See *Labor and Monoploly Capital* (New York: Monthly Review Press, 1974), esp., p. 87. (hereafter cited as *Labor*))

20. Lenin, *Selected Works*, pp. 332-333.

21. D. Gvishiani, *Organization and Management* (Moscow: Progress Publishers, 1972), pp. 26-28, 103, 175; V. G. Afanas'ev, "O soderzhanii (osnovykh funktsiyakh) upravleniya sotsialisticheskim obshchestvom" in his *Nauchnoe Upravlenie Obshchestvom* (Moscow: Misl', 1967), p. 26; P. A. Rachkov, *Rol'nauki v stroitel'stve kommunizma* (Moscow: Moscow University, 1969), pp. 187-190.

22. A. P. Volkov, "O merakh po uluchsheniyu organizatsii truda v promyshlennosti i stroitel'stve," *Sotsialisticheskii trud*, No. 9 (September 1965)

23. Afanas'ev, *op. cit.*, pp. 25, 26; V. A. Karpushin, *Nauchnyi kommunizm* (Moscow: Politicheskaya literatura, 1965), p. 216.
As an unsigned article entitled "NOT: Opyt i problemy" stated it: "Technological processes and equipment in the final account predetermine the components of the organization of labor and the condition for its application." In *Sotsialisticheskii trud*, No. 9 (September 1967)

24. Volkov, *op. cit.*, p. 5 (Volkov's italics)

25. Examples of Soviet efforts in the more narrow engineering vein (e.g., fitting men to machine processes, adjusting operations to new technology in the interest of greater productivity) would include: G. A. Prudenskii, *Vremya i trud* (Moscow: Misl', 1964); G. A. Krayukhin, *Effektivnost' proizvodstva i tekhnicheskii progress* (Leningrad: Lenizdat, 1973).

26. Volkov, *op. cit.*, p. 8.

27. Unsigned, "NOT: Opyt i problemy", *supra*, p. 93; see also Kh. Repp and I. Tamm, "Rabochee vremya," *Sovety deputatov trudyashchikhsya*, No. 9 (September 1969), pp. 69-75.

28. "NOT: Opyt i problemy," *supra*, pp. 90, 99.

29. *Kat organizovat' sorevnovanie?* (Pamphlet; Moscow: Politicheskaya literatura, 1969).

30. "NOT: Opyt i problemy," *supra*, p. 97. (author's italics)
31. *Izvestia* (May 14, 1977), p. 5.
32. *Izvestia* (March 23, 1977), p. 2.
33. "NOT: Opyt i problemy," *supra*, pp. 94-97.
34. *Ibid.*, pp. 98-101.
35. *Etika sovetskoi gosudarstvennoi sluzhby* (Moscow: Yuridicheskaya literatura, 1970), p. 18.
36. Volkov, *op. cit.*, p. 5. (Volkov's italics)
37. "NOT: Opyt i problemy," *supra*, pp. 93, 93, 99.
38. *Ibid.*, p. 99.
39. *Ibid.*, p. 107; I. L. Bachilo has put it this way: "Organizing the apparatus of administration, he [the *rukovoditel*] constantly has in mind, as the major organizing goal, the objectives of production. . . . In all cases, the final goal—production—remains foremost, but the relationship of elements and means of administration changes." See his "Organizatsiya truda sluzhashchikh" in *Sluzhashchii sovetskogo gosudarstvennogo apparata*, ed., Yu. A. Tikhomirov (Moscow: Yuridicheskaya literature, 1970)
40. "NOT: Opyt i problemy," *supra*, p. 21.
41. An offshot of *NOT* in the bureaucratic realm is *NOUT*, the scientific organization of administrative labor. Its general characteristics—rule-of-thumb, efficienty-oriented thinking, spiced with moral, altruistic, self-actualizing considerations—are the same as those of *NOT*. See V. I. Remnev, "Deyatel'nosti sluzhashchikh—nauchnye osnovi" in Tikhomirov, *op. cit.*, pp. 256-277; Gvishiani, *Organization and Management*, pp. 17-26.
42. Afanas'ev, *Nauchnoe upravlenie*, p. 3.
43. Gvishiani, *Organization and Management*, p. 28.
44. Rachkov, *Rd'nauki*, pp. 187-196.
45. Karpushin, *Nauchnyi Kommunizm*, pp. 224-229.
46. Juergen Habermas, *Towards a Rational Society* (London: Heinemann, 1971), p. 117.
47. Richard A. Johnson, et al, *The Theory and Management of Systems* (2nd ed.; New York: McGraw-Hill, 1967), p. 3.
48. Herbert A. Simon, *The New Science of Management Decision* (New York: Harper and Row, 1960), p. 15.(hereafter cited as *Management Decision)*
49. Robert Boguslaw, *The New Utopians* (Englewood Cliffs: Prentice-Hall, 1965), p. 3 and *passim*. It might be emphasized, here, that the "people as things" aspect of systems analysis is not a characterization which anyone need impose upon the systems perspective. It is implicit in systems methodology and explicitly recognized by systems advocates such as Charles W. Doud who observes that the systems approach to the human side of the organization simply means that the "objects processed are people." See "How the Personnel Function Looks from the Information Systems Approach," *Public Personnel Review*, vol. 29 (July 1968).
50. Luther Gulick and L. Urwick, eds., *Papers on the Science of Administration* (New York: Institute of Public Administration, Columbia University, 1937).

51. For an explanation of operations research, developed in Britain during World War II, see Stafford Beer, *Decision and Control* (London: John Wiley and Sons, 1966).

For a proposed application of operations research to society in general, see Olaf Helmer, *Social Technology* (New York: Basic Books, 1966).

Jack Byrd outlines the application of operations research to American public administration in *Operation Research Models for Public Administration* (Lexington, Mass: Lexington Books, 1975).

52. F. de P. Hanika, *New Thinking in Management* (London: Lyon Grant and Green, 1965).

53. Johnson, *et al, The Theory and Management of Systems*, p. 113. (Johnson's italics)

54. *Ibid.*, pp. 86-89.

55. Simon, *Management Decision*, p. 20.

56. *Ibid.* pp. 24-27.

For an outstanding critique of computer fetishism and the corresponding debasement of human beings, see Joseph Weizenbaum's *Computer Power and Human Reason* (San Francisco: W. H. Freeman, 1976).

57. C. R. Deckert, *The Social Impact of Cybernetics* (Notre Dame: Notre Dame University Press, 1966), pp. 11-37; esp., p. 28. (hereafter cited as *Cybernetics*)

For examples of the systems approach in American administrative literature, see Herbert Kaufman, *Administrative Feedback* (Washington, D.C.: The Brookings Institute, 1973); Kenneth S. Brown, "Management Science—Its Role in the Organization," *Managerial Planning*, vol. 21 (July/August 1972); Richard J. Tersine, "Organization Decision Theory—A synthesis," *Managerial Planning*, vol. 21 (July/August 1972); Roy Fenstermaker, "Management Systems Engineering," *Management Review*, vol. 58 (February 1969); Gilbert Burck, "The Age of the Computer," *Management Review*, vol. 53 (September 1964).

58. Maxim W. Makulak, "Cybernetics and Marxism Leninism" in Deckert, *Cybernetics*, pp. 129-159.

59. Rachkov, *Rol' nauki*, pp. 174-181.

60. A. Bezuglov, *Soviet Deputy* (Moscow: Progress Publishers, 1973), p. 119.

John J. Ford writes: "The methodological approaches [in the USSR] to the control of the new man's development are fundamentally the same as those that will be used in controlling the cybernetic factory." See "Soviet Cybernetics and Institutional Development" in Deckert, *Cybernetics*, pp. 161-192; esp., p. 183.

61. Peter C. Ludz, "Marxism and Systems Theory in a Bureaucratic Society," *Social Research*, vol. 42 (Winter 1975)

62. Paul Cocks, "Rethinking the Organizational Weapon: The Soviet System in a Systems Age," *World Politics*, vol. 32 (January 1980)

63. Stephen White, "Contradiction and Change in State Socialism," *Soviet Studies*, vol. 26 (January 1974)

64. D. M. Kruk, *Upravlenie obshchestvennym proizvodstvom pri sotsializme* (Moscow: Ekonomika, 1972), p. 73.

65. I. V. Blauberg and E. G. Yudin, "Sistemnyi podkhod v sotsial'nykh issledovaniyakh," *Voprosy filosofii*, No. 9 (1967), pp. 100-111; esp. p. 102.

66. Gvishiani, *Organization and Management*, p. 145.

For a soviet explanation of systems analysis which reads no differently from the common American version of same, see V. E. Adrianova, *Deyatel'nost' cheloveka v sistemakh upravleniya* (Leningrad: Leningrad University, 1974).

67. Deckert, *Cybernetics*, p. 16.

68. For an overview, see Raymond Bauer, ed., *Social Indicators* (Cambridge, Mass.: M.I.T. Press, 1966).

A Soviet version of social indicators appears in Afanas'ev, "Nauchnoe rukovodstvo sotsial'nymi protessami," *Kommunist*, No. 12 (August 1965).

69. Bendix, *Work and Authority*, pp. 326-327.

70. Peter F. Drucker, "Employee Education: A Realistic Goal?", *Management Review*, vol. 53 (March 1954).

For another American example of this outlook, see J. Douglas Brown, *The Human Nature of Organizations* (New York: AMACON, 1973), pp. 53-67.

For Soviet examples, see G. T. Zhuravlev, *Sotsial'naya informatsiya i upravlenie ideologicheskim protsessom* (Moscow: Misl', 1973); O. V. Kozlova, *Tekhnika, tekhnologiya i kadry upravleniva proizvodstvom* (Moscow: Ekonomika, 1973), pp. 59-67; Kruk, *op. cit.*, pp. 81, 82.

71. James Menzies Black, "Employee Communication: All Dressed Up and No Place to Go," *Management Review*, vol. 58 (July 1959)

72. Andre Gorz, "The Tyranny of the Factory: Today and Tomorrow," *Telos*, No. 16 (Summer 1973).

73. Summarized in Braverman, *Labor*, pp. 213-224.

74. Harley Shaiken, "Detroit Downsizes U.S. Jobs," *The Nation*, vol. 231 (October 1980).

The Soviets are busy copying these "advanced capitalist techniques." Deputy Director Zhurkin of the Institute of the USA and Canada in Moscow reported during a discussion in August 1979 that the Kama River Truck Factory, the USSR's largest single enterprise, duplicates in work layout and managerial structure that found among Detroit's "Big Three" automakers.

In general, see A. C. Sutton, *Western Technology and Soviet Economic Development* (3 vols.; Stanford: Stanford University Press, 1968, 1971, 1973).

75. P. M. Blau and R. A. Schoenherr, *The Structure of Organizations* (New York: Basic Books, 1971), esp., p. 77.

76. Robert Blauner, *Alienation and Freedom* (Chicago: The University of Chicago Press, 1964), pp. 167, 175-186.

Simon *Management Decison*, pp. 36-48. He offers a comprehensive statement of the technocratic credo on automation.

77. V. V. Poshataev, "Rol' i mesto nauchno-tekhnicheskoi revolyutsii v kommunisticheskom stroitel'stve," *Problemy nauchnogo kommunizma* ed., Afanas'ev (vol. 7; Moscow: Misl', 1973).

78. V. P. Korienko puts it thusly: "At the same level of technical develop-

ment, socialism, in comparison with capitalism, permits to an incomparably greater degree the utilization of the possibilities of machine production, the realization of which promotes the all-around development of the individual. In the conditions of socialism, technical advances are put into use which prevent or in each case mollify the negative aspects of the work regimen. So, the negative influence of the assembly line on the human organism is avoided in socialist production with the help of the technical norming of labor, the arranging of an obligatory time for rest, and also with the help of a high level of organizational safety in the work." See *Obshchestvennoe razdelenie truda* (Moscow: Ekonomicheskaya literatura, 1963), p. 47.

79. *Ibid.*, p. 197.

80. V. G. Afanas'ev, *Nauchnyi kommunizm* (2nd ed.; Moscow: Politizdat, 1969), pp. 249-252.

81. Karpushin, *Nauchnyi Kommunizm*, pp. 209-229.

82. Warren Bennis, "Organizational Change: Operating in the Temporary Society," *Management Review*, vol. 58 (August 1969).

83. On the consumption side, another American administrative writer, Allen Schick, has given an identical figure for what would be called "communist abundance" were the author living in the USSR. Since he is not, Shick uses the term "homogenous majority of affluents" to refer to eighty percent of the *present* US population. See "Systems Analysis and Systems Budgeting," *Public Administration Review*, vol. 29 (March/April 1969).

84. On the American side, this tendency is described by Bill Patry in "Taylorism Comes to the Social Services," *Monthly Review* (October 1978). For a Soviet statement on the automated administration of an automated society, see T. Kiselev, "Nauchnyi podkhod," *Sovety deputatov trudyashchikhsya* (January 1977).

85. Ida R. Hoos, *Systems Analysis in Public Policy* (Berkeley: University of California Press, 1972).

86. Robert Lilienfeld, "Systems Theory as an Ideology," *Social Research*, vol. 42 (Winter 1975).

87. *The Juggernauts* (New York: Bobbs-Merrill, 1971), Chapter 7.

88. I. L. Horowitz and J. E. Katz, *Social Science and Public Policy in the United States* (New York: Praeger, 1975).

89. Two studies which point up the importance of "scientific" appearances in the making of personnel decisions which, as operational questions, have nothing whatever to do with science-based determinations are: Harrison M. Trice, James Belasco and Joseph Alutto, "The Role of Ceremonials in Organizational Behavior," *Industrial and Labor Relations Review*, vol. 23 (October 1969) and C. Sofer and M. Tuchman, "Appraisal Interviews and the Structure of Colleague Relations," *The Sociological Review*, vol. 18 (1970).

5. Ideologies of Administrative Leadership: "Humane" Administration

1. Robert W. Burgess, "Research for General Administration," *Scientific Management in American Industry*, ed., H. S. Person (New York: Harper and Brothers, 1929) (hereafter cited as *Scientific Management*)

2. See Vladimir Andrle, *Managerial Power in the Soviet Union* (Westmead, U.K.: Saxon House, 1976), pp. 116-133.

3. Barry M. Richman, *Management Development and Education in the Soviet Union* (East Lansing: Michigan State University, International Business Studies, 1967).

4. Quoted in Galina Sorokina's "Sovetnik direktora," *Literaturnaya gazeta* No. 6 (February 1975). (Sorokina's italics)

5. D. M. Gvishiani, *Organization and Management* (Moscow: Progress Publishers, 1972), pp. 16-17.

6. Take, for example, some comments made on this subject by the Communist Party's General Secretary, L. I. Brezhnev. In March 1968, Brezhnev remarked that the "Party has nurtured and put forward to the leadership of Party and State activities and the economy various highly qualified people, energetic workers who are devoted to the cause of communism, who enjoy the meritorious authority and esteem of working people. It can boldly be stated that we never had such qualified leading cadres as we do now." (*Izvestia*, March 30, 1968). In June of 1970, he went so far as to claim that: "The science of victory [in building communism] is, in essence, the science of management" (*Pravda*, June 13, 1970, quoted by Paul Cocks, "Rethinking the Organizational Weapon: The Soviet System in a Systems Age," *World Politics*, vol. 32 (January 1980), p. 229.)

7. Person, *Scientific Management*, pp. 427-439; esp., p. 432. (Person's italics)

8. Warren G. Bennis, *The Planning of Change* (New York: Holt, Rinehart and Winston, 1961), pp. 435-445; esp., p. 441.

9. Philip Selznick, *Leadership and Administration* (New York: Harper and Row, 1957). More recently, see "Corporate Values and Business Efficiency," *Management Review*, vol. 58 (June 1969).

10. *Ibid.*, pp. 14, 151, 152; William J. Gore, *Administrative Decision-Making* (New York: John Wiley and Sons, 1964), pp. 20, 21.

11. March and Simon, *Organizations*, pp. 65-67.

12. Chester A. Barnard, *The Functions of the Executive* (Cambridge: Harvard University Press, 1958), p. 279.

For more pedestrian accounts of "creative leadership" see Alex F. Osborn, "The Missing Link in Management," *Management Review*, vol. 53, (January 1954); Eugene Raudsepp, "On Becoming More Creative," *Management Review*, vol. 58 (August 1959).

13. J. Douglas Brown, *The Human Nature of Organizations* (New York: AMACON, 1973), pp. 19-29.

14. Joseph R. Coupal, "Where Are We? Where Are We Going?", *Public Management* vol. 48 (December 1966).

15. Thomas J. Davy, "The Administrative Policy-Making Officer," *Public Management*, vol. 39 (November 1957).

16. Harry Levinson, "Whatever Happened to Loyalty?", *Public Management*, vol. 48 (June 1966).

17. George E. Spaulding, "The 'Effective' Executive," *Management Review*, vol. 53 (November 1964).

18. Davy, "The Administrative Policy-Making Officer."
19. Warren G. Bennis, "Organizational Change: Operating in the Temporary Society," *Management Review*, vol. 58 (August 1969) and, idem, "The Leader of the Future," *Public Management*, vol. 52 (March 1970).
20. Michael G. Blansfield, "The Climate of Employee Development," *Management Review*, vol. 53 (January 1954). (Blansfield's italics)
21. D. M. Kruk, *Upravlenie obshchestvennym proizvodstvom pri sotsialisme* (Moscow: Ekonomika, 1972), p. 120. (Kruk's italics)
22. L. I. Umanskii, "V. I. Lenin ob organizatorskoi deyatel'nosti i organizatorskihk sposobnostykh," *Voprosy psikhologii*, No. 2 (March/April 1963).
23. V. M. Manokhin, *Sovetskaya gosudarstvennaya sluzhba* (Moscow: Yuridicheskaya literatura, 1966), p. 91.
24. V. D. Popkov, *Etika sovetskoi gosudarstvennoi sluzhby* (Moscow: Yuridicheskaya literatura, 1970), pp. 5, 10.
25. Ya. Fomenko, "Kollektivnost'—vysshii printsip rukovodsta," *Sovety deputatov trudyashchikhsya*, No. 12 (December 1964).
26. I. Ya. Kasitskii, "Vazhneishie cherty sovetskogo stilya khozyaistvennogo rukovodstvo," in *Problemy nauchnoi organizatsii upravleniya sotsialisticheskoi promyshlennostyu*, ed., D. M. Gvishiani (Moscow: Ekonomika, 1968).
27. *Ibid*, p. 235.
28. V. G. Afanas'ev, *Nauchnyi kommunizm* (2nd ed.; Moscow: Politizdat, 1969), p. 209. (Afanas'ev's italics)
29. Popkov, *Etika*, p. 85.
30. V. Maslov, "Nauka upravleniya i podgotovka rukovoditelei," *Ekonomicheskie nauki*, No. 1 (1970).
31. *Ibid.*, pp. 69, 70.
32. Popkov, *Etika*, p. 90.
33. N. I. Lapin, *Rukovoditel' kollektiva* (Moscow: Politicheskaya literatura, 1974), pp. 22, 23, 30, 31.
34. P. Masherov, "Stil' rukovodstva i vospitanie kadrov," *Kommunist*, No. 11 (July 1965).
35. Gviashini, *Organization and Management*, pp. 134-136.
36. See the front page editorial in *Izvestia* (April 9, 1977).
37. *Izvestia* (May 14, 1977), p. 5; *Izvestia* (March 16, 1977), p. 2.
38. *Izvestia* (January 6, 1977), p. 2; *Izvestia* (June 4, 1978), p. 2; *Izvestia* (September 19, 1978), p. 2.
39. Lapin, *Rudovoditel' kollektiva*, pp. 24-28; Popkov, *Etika*, pp. 132, 133. For an American equivalent, see James Owens, "What Kind of Leader Do They Follow?", *Management Review*, vol. 62 (April 1973).
40. Elton Mayo, *The Human Problems of an Industrial Civilization* (2nd ed.; Boston: Graduate School of Business Administration, Harvard University, 1946), p. 116. (hereafter cited as *Human Problems)*
41. *Ibid.*, p. 78.
42. W. J. Dickson and F. J. Roethlisberger, *Counseling in an Organization* (Cambridge, Mass.: Harvard University Press, 1966), chapter 9; esp., p. 208. (hereafter cited as *Counseling)*
43. Hedy Brown, "The Individual in the Organization," *Control and*

Ideology in Organizations, eds., Graeme Salaman and Kenneth Thompson (Cambridge: Mass.: MIT Press, 1980), p. 153. (hereafter cited as *Control*)

44. J. Carpentier, "Organizational Techniques and the Humanization of Work," *International Labor Review*, vol. 110 (August 1974).

45. Mayo believed that the major problem in the industrial society of the United States was "the misunderstanding between employers and workers." *Human Problems*, p. 177.

46. For instance, see Bob Hoke, "The Game of Work: Key to On-the-Job Behavior," *Management Review*, vol. 58 (December 1969).

47. For a description of this strategy, see Dickson and Roethlisberger, *Counseling*, pp. 19-36, 355-356.

48. *Ibid.*, esp. pp. 36-45 and Chapter 3.

49. *Ibid.*, pp. 250-254.

50. *Ibid.*, pp. 273-276.

51. *Ibid.*, chapter 7.

52. Robert Dubin, *Human Relations in Administration* (Englewood Cliffs: Prentice-Hall, 1968), pp. 449-463.

53. Harry Calvert Krueger, "Some Thoughts On Human Relations in Budgeting," *Managerial Planning*, vol. 20 (November/December 1971).

54. Thomas G. Spates, "Human Relations: How Far Have We Come?", *Management Review*, vol. 58 (September 1959).

55. Nina Bogomolova, *"Human Relations" Doctrine: Ideological Weapon of the Monopolies* (Moscow: Progress Publishers, 1973).

56. Selznick, *Leadership and Administration*, puts the matter in a fashion representative of American authors. "As human beings," he writes, "and not as mere tools, they [employees] have their own needs for self-protection and self-fulfillment—needs that may either sustain or undermine it [the formal organization]. These human relations are a great reservoir of energy. They may be directed in constructive ways toward desired ends or they may become recalcitrant sources of frustration. One objective of sound management practice is to direct and control these internal social pressures."

57. March and Simon, *Organizations*, remark that "one problem in organizing control systems in complex organizations is to neutralize or eliminate the dysfunctional consequences of subgroup organization without destroying its ability to perform necessary functions."

Similarly, Barnard *(Functions of the Executive*, p. 42) argues that "the group compels changes in the psychological character of the individual and, therefore, in the motives of individuals, which otherwise would not take place. So far as these changes are in a direction favorable to the cooperative system, the group is a resource. So far as they are unfavorable, the group is a limitation."

58. See their "O nekotorykh sotsial'no-psikhologicheskykh aspektakh upravleniya proizvodstvom" in Gvishiani, *Problemy Nauchnoi*, pp. 243-255.

59. B. D. Levin and M. N. Perfil'ev, *Kadry apparata upravleniya v SSSR* (Leningrad: Nauka, 1970), p. 52.

60. Popkov, *Etika*, pp. 45-47.

61. *Ibid.*, pp. 135-136.

62. See Alex Carey, "The Hawthorne Studies: A Radical Criticism," *American Sociological Review*, vol. 32 (June 1967).

63. Bendix, *Work and Authority*, pp. 288-297.

64. Unsigned, "Raising Employee Productivity," *Management Review*, vol. 58 (February 1959).

65. Maslow's ideas are elaborated in *Motivation and Personality* (New York: Harper and Row, 1954); and, idem, *Toward a Psychology of Being* (Princeton: D. Van Nostrand, 1962).

66. See Maslow's *Eupsychian Management* (Homewood, Ill.: Richard D. Irwin, 1965).

76. William Leiss, *The Limits to Satisfaction* (Toronto: Toronto University Press, 1976), pp. 55-58.

68. See Hedy Brown, in Salaman and Thompson, *Control*, pp. 155-159.

69. David Schuman, *Bureaucracies, Organizations and Administration* (New York: Macmillan, 1976), pp. 113-117.

70. Peter F. Drucker, *The Society* (New York: Harper and Brothers, 1950), pp. 157-162, esp., p. 165. (Drucker's italics)

71. Peter F. Drucker, *The Practice of Management* (New York: Harper and Brothers, 1954), p. 5.

72. For some examples of more recent applications of management by objectives, see James C. Febray, "Planning that Begins and Ends with People," *Management Review*, vol. 62 (January 1973) and Edwin L. Miller, "Selection by Objectives: A Function of the Management by Objectives Philosophy," *Public Personnel Review*, vol. 29 (April 1968).

Edward C. Schleh candidly echos Drucker's outlook in noting that although it is indeed management which sets the objectives, "it is usually best to get the man [who is to meet the objectives] to participate in setting his own objectives. This tends to sell him on the fairness of the objectives, helps him to understand them better and develops his incentive to meet them." See "Management by Objectives: Some Principles for Making it Work," *Management Review*, vol. 58 (November 1959).

73. R. S. Ritchie, "An Evolution of the Practice of Management," *Peter Drucker: Contribution to Business Management*, eds., T. H. Bonaparte and J. E. Flaherty (New York: New York University Press, 1970), pp. 82-92.

74. Drucker, *Practice of Management*, p. 129.

75. *Ibid.*, pp. 262-269.

76. *Ibid.*, p. 136.

77. *Ibid.*, p. 268

Herbert A. Simon has developed a similar management strategy. For instance, in *Public Administration* (New York: Alfred A. Knopf, 1958), he proposed that: "Restriction of output is the result of real or fancied conflict between the goals or values of a work group and the goals or values of the larger organization" (p. 115). The point, then, is to replace conflict with conformity, by structuring the situation such that the subordinate "is expected to ask himself, 'How would my superior wish me to behave under these circumstances?' " See Simon, *Administrative Behavior* (2nd ed.; New York, Macmillan, 1960), p. 129.

78. Douglas McGregor, *The Human Side of Enterprise* (New York: McGraw-Hill, 1960).

79. W. G. Bennis and E. H. Schein, eds., *Leadership and Motivation*, (Cambridge, Mass.: MIT Press, 1966), p. 15 (emphasis in original).

80. *Ibid.*, p. 132.

81. *Ibid.*, p. 215.

82. *Ibid.*, pp. 253-257.

83. *Ibid.*, p. 262.

84. *Ibid.*, p. 266.

85. See, in general, the following: Stephen M. Corey, *Action Research to Improve School Practices* (New York: Columbia University, Teachers College, 1953); idem, *Helping Other People Change* (Columbus: Ohio State University Press, 1963); and with Gordon N. Mackenzie, *Instructional Leadership* (New York: Columbia Teacher's College, 1954); R. P. Biller, "Converting Knowledge into Action: The Dilemma and Opportunity of the Post-Industrial Society" (mimeo; University of Southern California, October 25, 1969).

86. R. R. Blake and J. S. Mouton, *Group Dynamics—Key to Decision Making* (Houston: Gulf Publishing Company, 1961).

87. See, in particular, Chris Argyris, *Management and Organizational Development* (New York: McGraw-Hill, 1971) and idem, *Understanding Organizational Behavior* (Homewood, Ill.: Dorsey Press, 1960).

88. William J. Crockett, "For Those Who Want to Take Organizational Development Seriously," *Management Review*, vol. 62 (June 1973). See also, Melvin Sorcher and Herbert H. Meyers, "Increasing Motivation in the Plant," *Management Review*, vol. 58 (January 1969).

89. Crockett, "For Those Who Want to Take Organizational Development Seriously," pp. 13-19; esp. p. 19.

90. Robert R. Blake and Jane A. Mouton, "A Behavioral Science Design for the Development of Society," *The Journal of Applied Behavioral Science*, vol. 7 (March/April 1971).

91. As Argyris, rather off-handedly, has remarked: "The basic motivation a scientist has toward his work is the desire to understand (and as a result predict and control) the phenomena upon which he is focusing." See his *Understanding Organizational Behavior*, p. 30.

92. *Inter alia*, Philip R. Harris, "Facing the Realities of Change," *Management Review*, vol. 58 (July 1969), and Matthias E. Lukens, "What's Ahead in Management?", *Public Management*, vol. 39 (December 1957).

93. Phillip L. Hunsaker et al, "Assessing and Developing Administrators for Turbulent Environments," *Administration and Society*, vol. 7 (November 1975).

94. Blake and Mouton, "A Behavioral Science Design,"

95. *Ibid.*

96. See, for instance, Paul Pigors and Charles A. Myers, "In Short:

Personnel Administration for Line Managers," *People in Public Service*, eds., Robert T. Golembiewski and Michael Cohen (Itasca, Ill.: F. E. Peacock, 1970), pp. 434-452; and, in the same volume, the article, "The Triumph of Technique over Purpose," by Wallace A. Sayre, pp. 460-464.

97. Mauk Mulder, "Power Equalization through Participation?", *Administrative Sciences Quarterly*, vol. 16 (March 1971).

98. Dorwin Cartwright, "Achieving Change in People," in Bennis, *The Planning of Change*, pp. 702-704; Edward J. Green, "Decisions-Commitments-Results," *Managerial Planning*, vol. 20 (May/June 1972).

99. March and Simon, *Organizations*, p. 54.

100. Cartwright in Bennis, *The Planning of Change*, p. 701.

101. Bruce G. Lawson, "Employee Attitude Surveys: An Aid to Administrators," *Public Personnel Review*, vol. 30 (April 1969).

102. Penelope Wong, Michael Doyle and David Strass, "Problem Solving Through 'Process Management' ", *Management Review*, vol. 62 (November 1973).

103. Maslov, *Nauka upravleniya*, p. 67. Gore's ideas appear in his *Administrative Decision-Making* (New York: John Wiley, 1964).

104. A. M. Omarova, *Nauchnye osnovy upravleniya sotsialisticheskoi ekonomikoi* (Moscow: Misl', 1973), pp. 105-106.

105. *Ibid.*, pp. 100-103; Afanas'ev in *Nauchnoe upravlenie obshchestvom*, pp. 10-15.

106. Popkov, *Etika*, p. 10.

107. Rachkov, *Rol' nauki*, p. 196; Omarova, *Nauchnyi osnovy*, p. 97.

108. Afanas'ev, *Nauchnyi kommunizm*, esp., pp. 327-395.

109. Omarova, *Nauchnyi osnovy*, pp. 94, 95. According to B. A. Gryaznov, Party administrators use the same approach via the Party member(s) within a given work group. See *Organizatsionno-Partiinaya rabota: problemy i opyt* (Moscow: Moskovskii rabochii, 1974), pp. 172-174.

110. Popkov, *Etika*, pp. 45-54, esp. p. 54.

111. *Ibid.*, pp. 94, 05.

112. Yu A. Rozenbaum, "Etikopsikhologicheskie voprosy v rabote gosudarstvennikh sluzhashchikh," Tikhomirov, *op. cit.*, pp. 208-213. Rozenbaum (pp. 205-207) predicates this tactic upon its alleged success in channeling the dynamics of informal groups into the fulfillment of organizational tasks.

See also, Manokhin, *Sovetskaya gosudarstvennoi sluzhby*, esp., pp. 180-188.

113. Examples of such "participatory" decision-making practices in the Soviet literature on administration include: Yu. A. Tikhomirov, "Razvitie demokraticheskikh osnov organizatsii i deyatel'nosti" in *Mestnye sovety na sovremennom etape*, eds. D. A. Gaidukov and N. G. Starovoitov (Moscow: Nauka, 1965), pp. 11-13, 41, 46. A. Lashin, "Massy upravlyaut," *Sovety deputatov trudyashchikhsya*, No. 9 (September 1966); A. Savko, "Mestnye sovety i obshchestvenniye samodeyatel'nye organizatsii," *Byulleten' Ispolnitel'nogo Komiteta Moskovskogo Gorodskogo Soveta deputatov trudyashchikhsya*, No. 17 (September 1970).

114. Omarova, *Nauchnye osnovy*, p. 98.
115. Rachkov, *Rol'nauki*, p. 155; Afanas'ev, *Nauchnyi kommunizm*, pp. 272-275.
116. Karpushin *Nauchnyi kommunizm*, pp. 230-235.
117. A. Kh. Verzikhov, in "NOT: Opyt i problemy," *Sotsialisticheskii trud*, No. 9 (September 1969), p. 53.
118. Rachkov, *Rol'nauki*, p. 140, 159-163.
119. *Ibid.*, p. 11. (Rachkov's italics).
120. Maslov, *Nauka upravaleniya*, pp. 70-72.
121. S. P. Trapeznikov, "Razvitie obshchestvennykh nauk i povyshenie ikh roli v kommunisticheskom stroitel'stve," *Voprosy filosofii*, No. 12 (1967), pp. 3-27; Umanskii, *Lenin*, pp. 14, 15; Omarova, *Nauchnye, osnovy*, pp. 94, 95.
122. L. A. Sergienko and A. S. Kokovin, "Prokhoshdenie gosudarstvennoi sluzhby" in Tikhomirov, *Sluzhashchii*, pp. 60-94; esp., p. 65.
123. This term is not intended to suggest that practitioners are only interested in results (they may or may not be, I do not know). Rather, it is employed to convey the ideological form and content of the dominant pattern of their responses during the interviews, that is, the connotation of special knowledge.

6. Ideologies of Democratic Bureaucracy in the United States

1. Dwight Waldo, *The Administrative State* (New York: Roland Press, 1948).
2. J. M. Pfiffner heralded the advent of just such a group "who possess the just, wise and omniscient qualities of Plato's guardians" in *Research Methods in Public Administration* (New York: Roland Press, 1940), p. 25.
3. Waldo, *The Administrative State*, pp. 27-33.
4. Christopher Lasch, "Democracy and the 'Crisis of Confidence,' " *Democracy*, vol. 1 (January 1981).
5. David Dickson, "Limiting Democracy: Technocrats and the Liberal State," *Democracy*, vol. 1 (January 1981).
6. M. J. Crozier, S. P. Huntington and J. Watanuki, *The Crisis of Democracy* (New York: New York University Press, 1975), pp. 114, 162-163.
7. C. A. Harrell and D. G. Weiford, "The City Manager and the Policy Process," *Public Administration Review*, vol. 19 (Spring 1959).
8. Quoted in Dickson, "Limiting Democracy," p. 62.
9. E.g., Allen Schick, "Systems Politics and Systems Budgeting," *Public Administration Review*, vol. 29 (March/April 1969).
10. George E. Berkley, *The Administrative Revolution* (Englewood Cliffs, New Jersey: Prentice Hall, 1971), p. 145.
11. Herbert A. Simon et. al, *Public Administration* (New York: Alfred A. Knopf, 1958), p. 322.

12. Eugene P. Drovin and Robert H. Simmons, *From Amoral to Humane Bureaucracy* (San Francisco: Canfield, 1972), p. 37 (hereafter cited as *Humane Bureaucracy*).

13. *Ibid.*, p. 28.

14. Dwight Waldo, "Scope and Theory of Public Administration," *Theory and Practice of Public Administration*, ed., James C. Charlesworth (Monograph No. 8; Philadelphia: American Academy of Political Science, 1968), p. 26. (Waldo's italics)

15. Victor Thompson coined this expression in *Modern Organizations* (New York: Knopf, 1961). He traces its causes to the fact that "Bureaucratic culture makes certain demands upon clients as well as upon organizational employees. There are people in our society who have not been able to adjust to these demands. To them bureaucracy is a curse. . . . This kind of behavior is external to the organization, and is not simply a reaction to bureaupathology. Its source is to be found within the critic himself, not with the organization."

One who has the "social disease," says Thompson, "has low powers of abstraction" and is likely to "fear bureaucracy because [he] cannot personalize it." (pp. 170-173)

16. For a synopsis of this viewpoint in the professional literature prior to 1940, see Waldo, *The Administrative State*, pp. 90-101.

It would appear that this governing class has not always been too fussy about the sources from which it has drawn "principles" of governing. A. H. Leighton, for instance, derived a set of such principles for administrators, aimed essentially at preventing open conflicts and "managing change," from his observations of a WW II Japanese "relocation camp." See Leighton's *The Governing of Man: General Principles and Recommendations Based on Experience at a Japanese Relocation Camp* (New York: Octagon Books, 1964).

17. Quoted in Dvorin and Simmons, *Humane Bureaucracy*, p. 2.

18. Waldo in Charlesworth, *Theory and Practice of Public Administration*, p. 10. It is interesting to note that, when asked in discussion on his paper, as to what he means by "profession" in the context of public administration, Waldo simply replied that he did not know.

19. See, *inter alia*, Samuel Haber, *Efficiency and Uplift* (Chicago: The University of Chicago Press, 1964); Martin Schiesl, *The Politics of Efficiency* (Berkeley: University of California Press, 1977).

20. *Inter alia*, James Weinstein, *The Corporate Ideal in the Liberal State* (Boston: Beacon, 1968).

21. Harry A. Toulmin, *The City Manager* (New York: D. Appleton and Co., 1917), pp. 13-14.

22. Richard S. Childs, *Civic Victories* (New York: Harper and Brothers, 1952), p. 141. Don K. Price remarks that "a businessman of importance could not be induced to take part in 'politics,' but he might be drafted for a position on the municipal council if he were assured that the municipality

was to be managed like a business corporation." See Price's "The Promotion of the City Manager Plan," *Public Opinion Quarterly*, vol. 15 (Winter 1941).

23. Clinton R. Woodruff, *City Government by Commission* (New York: D. Appleton and Co., 1911), p. 253.

24. Toulmin, *The City Manager*, p. 51

25. Leonard D. White, *The City Manager* (Chicago: The University of Chicago Press, 1927), pp. 295-298.

26. See, for example, Samuel P. Hays, "The Politics of Reform in Municipal Government in the Progressive Era," *Pacific Northwest Quarterly*, vol. 55 (October 1964); C. N. Glaab and T. A. Brown, *History of Urban America* (New York: Macmillan, 1967), pp. 181-215.

27. I. B. Helburn and D. T. Barnum, "Making Personnel Decisions by Public Referenda," *Public Personnel Management*, vol. 7 (March-April 1978).

28. Frederick C. Mosher, *Democracy and the Public Service* (New York: Oxford University Press, 1968), pp. 209-218. (hereafter cited as Public Service)

29. Dvorin and Simmons, *Humane Bureaucracy*, p. 9.

30. See, for instance, Keith F. Mulrooney, "Prologue: Can City Managers Deal Effectively with Major Social Problems?", *Public Administration Review*, vol. 31 (January/February 1971).

31. Dwight Waldo, "Public Administration in a Time of Revolutions," *Public Administrtion Review*, vol. 28 (July/August 1968).

32. H. George Frederickson, "Toward a New Public Administration," *Toward a New Public Administration: The Minnowbrook Perspective*, ed., Frank Marini (Scranton: Chandler Publishing Co., 1971), p. 312. (Frederickson's italics) (hereafter cited as *Minnowbrook Perspectives)*

33. Todd R. LaPorte has stated it this way: "Our primary normative premise should be that *the purpose of public organization is the reduction of economic, social and psychic suffering and the enhancement of life opportunities for those inside and outside the organization* . . . [P]ublic organizations should be assessed in terms of their effect upon the production and distribution of material abundance in efforts to free all people from economic deprivation and want . . . [P]ublic organizations have a responsibility to enhance social justice by freeing their participants and the citizenry to decide their own way and by increasing the probability of shared political and social privilege . . . [T]he quality of personal encounter and increasing possibilities of personal growth should be elevated to major criteria in organizational assessment." See LaPorte's "The Recovery of Relevance in the Study of Public Organization," Marini, *Minnowbrook Perspective*, p. 32. (LaPorte's italics)

34. Michael M. Harmon, "Normative Theory and Public Administration: Some suggestions for a Redefinition of Administrative Responsibility," Marini, *Minnowbrook Perspective*, pp. 172-185; esp. p. 179.

35. Mosher, *Public Service*, p. 3.

36. Orion S. White, "The Concept of Administrative Praxis," *Journal of Comparative Administration*, vol. 5 (May 1973).

37. Quoted in Donald C. Wagner, "Management's Social Responsibility," *Public Management*, vol. 39 (December 1957). (Wagner's italics)

38. E.g., Arthur W. Bromage, "Managers Become More Oriented to Human Values," *Public Management*, vol. 47 (October 1965).

39. Wallace G. Lonergan, "The Management Role in Community Development," *Public Management*, vol. 48 (January 1966). As if to assuage those suffering from "bureausis," Lonergan adds that the "leadership role of the city manager is sometimes viewed uneasily, for it seems undemocratic for an unelected official to provide leadership. However, this suggests need for a clearer understanding of the role in modern complex systems under pressure to change."

40. Robert P. Biller, "Some Implications of Adaptation Capacity for Organizational and Political Development," Marini, *Minnowbrook Perspective*, p. 118.

41. Orion S. White, "Social Change and Administrative Adaption," *Ibid.*, pp. 80-82.

42. Duane Lockard, "The City Manager, Administrative Theory and Political Power," *Political Science Quarterly*, vol. 77 (June 1962) (hereafter cited as "Political Power")

43. Harold Stone, Don K. Price and K. H. Stone, *City Manager Government in the United States* (Chicago: Public Administration Service, 1940), pp. 248-249.

44. Leonard White, *The City Manager*, pp. 212, 213, 295-298, 301. This view has not gone completely out of fashion. E.g., Carleton F. Sharpe, "The Past—A Challenge to the Future," *Public Management*, vol. 40 (December 1958).

45. Lockard, "Political Power," pp. 228-230.

46. R. P. Boynton, "Mayor-Manager Relationships in Large Council-Manager Cities: A Reinterpretation," *Public Administration Review*, vol. 31, (January/February 1971).

47. Henry Reining, "The City Manager as Urban Coordinator," *Public Management*, vol. 43 (June 1961) (hereafter cited as "Urban Coordinator")

48. In particular, Clarence E. Ridley, *The Role of the City Manager in Policy Formulation* (Chicago: The International City Manager's Association, 1958). (hereafter cited as *Policy Formulation*)

49. Reining, "Urban Coordinator," pp. 126-129, *passim*; David S. Brown, "The Ultimate Managerial Challenge—Creating Change," *Public Management*, vol. 45 (December 1963); Desmond L. Anderson, "Achieving Community Consensus," *Public Management*, vol. 48 (March 1966).

50. Clarence E. Ridley and O. F. Nolting, *The City-Manager Profession* (Chicago: The University of Chicago Press, 1934).

51. John M. Pfiffner, "The Job of the City Manager," *Public Management*, vol. 43 (June 1961).

52. Thomas W. Fletcher, "What is the Future of Our Cities and the City Manager?", *Public Administration Review*, vol. 31 (January/February 1971).

53. "How Manager Leads," *National Civic Review*, vol. 50 (June 1961).

54. Ridley, *Policy Formulation*, pp. 28-29.

55. Jeptha J. Carrell, "The Role of the City Manager: A Survey Report," *Public Management*, vol. 44 (April 1962).

56. Quoted in Ridley, *Policy Formulation*, p. 15.

57. Walter H. Wheeler, "Management for Freedom," *Management Review* vol. 53 (February 1954); and, Wayne G. Broehl, "Management Faces Its Critics," *Management Review* vol. 58 (November 1959); John J. Corson, "Government and Business—Partners in the Space Age," *Management Review* vol. 58 (August 1959); James C. Worthy, "A Political Philosophy for the Businessman," *Management Review* vol. 58 (October 1959); Ralph J. Cordiner, "Corporate Citizenship and the Businessman," *Management Review* vol. 58 (July 1959); Gerald R. Rosen, "Corporations, Employees, and Politics," *Management Review* vol. 53 (July 1964).

58. Marion B. Folsom, *Executive Decision Making* (New York: McGraw Hill, 1962), pp. 132-137; esp., p. 132.

59. Sharpe, "The Past," p. 285.

60. Randy H. Hamilton, "Bridging the Gap Between Citizens and City Government," *Emerging Patterns of Urban Administration*, eds., G. F. Brown and T. P. Murphy (Lexington, Mass.: D. C. Heath, 1970), pp. 64-76. (hereafter cited as *Emerging Patterns*)

61. Eugene I. Johnson, "People Greatest Asset in Building Better Cities," *Public Management*, vol. 47 (May 1965); Julian Wise, "Making PR Part of the Management Team," *Public Management*, vol. 52 (December 1970).

62. Timothy W. Costello, "The Change Process in Municipal Government," Brown and Murphy, *Emerging Patterns*, pp. 13-32.

63. In Marini, *Minnowbrook Perspective*, pp. 118-127.

64. Berkley, *The Administrative Revolution*, pp. 118-127.

65. Robert L. Williams, "The Planning Role in Urban Decision Making," Brown and Murphy, *Emerging Patterns*, p. 127.

T. M. Hennessey and B. G. Peters have, I think, quite correctly called attention to the anti-democratic nature of "advocacy planning" in noting that "such reforms render representative institutions 'remote' from the citizenry, thereby raising the 'price' (i.e., difficulty) of political participation, and thereby reducing probabilities of obtaining adequate information on the changing preferences of citizens." See their "Political Paradoxes in Postindustrialism: A Political Economy Perspective," *Policy Studies Journal*, vol. 3 (Spring 1975).

66. Esp., Schick, *op.cit.*

67. Quoted by Ida Hoos in *Systems Analysis in Public Policy* (Berkley: University of California Press, 1972), p. 171. (Author's italics)

68. Bruce L. Gates "Needs-Based Budgeting: Considerations of Effectiveness, Efficiency and Justice in the Delivery of Human Services." (Paper delivered at the 1975 Annual Meeting of the American Political Science Association, San Francisco, California, September 2-5, 1975).

69. Warren G. Bennis, *The Planning of Change* (Holt, Rinehart and Winston, 1961), pp. 1-6.

70. E.g., Orin F. Nolting, "Managers Must Be Cognizant of Change Factors," *Public Management*, vol. 47 (November 1965), pp. 280-283; and, in the December number of the same volume, Charles N. Kimball, "Time for Cities to Use Space Age Techniques," Wallace G. Lonergan, "The Management of Change" (pp. 305-309).

The notion that increased control is needed to protect freedom is put forward by William O. Stanley, "The Collapse of Automatic Adjustment," in Bennis, *The Planning of Change*, pp. 28-34.

71. Deckert, *Cybernetics*, p. 31.

72. On this topic, see Murray Edelman, *Political Language* (New York: Academic Press, 1977), esp., p. 93.

73. Gerth and Mills, *Weber*, esp. pp. 183, 226.

7. Administrative Communism in the Soviet Union

1. Lenin's well-known innovation was first put forth in 1902, in *What Is to Be Done?* (New York: International Publishers, 1969).

The best Western commentaries on Lenin's conception of the Party known to me are: Alfred G. Meyer, *Leninism* (New York: Praeger, 1962), pp. 19-91; George Lichtheim, *Marxism* (2nd ed.; London: Routledge and Kegan Paul, 1964), pp. 325-351.

2. Quoted in Merle Fainsod's *How Russia Is Ruled* (rev. ed.; Cambridge, Mass.: Harvard University Press, 1967), p. 249.

3. N. V. Barsukov and M. P. Karpov, *Partiinyi kontrol' deyatel'nosti administratsii* (Moscow: Politizdat, 1973), p. 3. The second quotation is from V. M. Chkhikvadze, *The Soviet Form of Popular Government* (Moscow: Progress Publishers, 1972), p. 69.

4. V. D. Popkov, *Etika sovetskoi gosudarstvennoi sluzhby* (Moscow: Yuridicheskaya literatura, 1970), p. 69.

5. V. A. Karpushin, *Nauchnyi kommunizm* (Moscow: Politicheskaya literatura, 1965), p. 313.

6. V. G. Afanas'ev, "O soderzhanii (osnovykh funktsiyakh) upravlenie sotsialisticheskim obshchestvom" in his *Nauchnoe upravlenie obshchestvom* (Moscow: Misl', 1967).

See also the unsigned article "Partiya vedet k kommunizmu," *Sovety deputatov trudyashchikhsya*, No. 5 (May 1971).

7. M. N. Marchenko, *Demokraticheskie osnovy politicheskoi organizatsii sovetskogo obshchestvo* (Moscow: Moscow State University, 1977), pp. 152-177, esp., p. 156.

8. B. Lazarev and A. Luk'yanov, "Vlast demokratiya, samoupravlenie," *Sovety deputatov trudyashchikhsya*, No. 12 (December 1964).

9. V. G. Afanas'ev, *Nauchnyi kommunizm* (2nd ed.; Moscow: Politizdat, 1969), pp. 297-98; for a tribute to the altruistic nature of party members, see pp. 104-115; see, also, A. I. Lepeshkin, *Sovety-Vlast' trudyashchikhsya 1917-1936* (Moscow: Yuridicheskaya literatura, 1967), pp. 18-26.

166   *The Ideology of Administration*

10. B. A. Gryaznov, *Organizatsionno-partiinaya rabota: problemy i opty* (Moscow: Moskovskii rabochii, 1974), p. 3.

11. P. A. Rachkov, *Rol' nauki v stroitel'stve kommunizma* (Moscow: Moscow University, 1969), p. 3.

12. Karpushin, *Nauchnyi kommunizm,* pp. 63-83; Afanas'ev, *Nauchnyi kommunizm,* pp. 55-58, 66.

13. Karpushin, *Nauchnyi kommunizm,* p. 3.

14. For an account of direct Party involvement in the governing process which, by Soviet standards, is exceptionally candid, see M. Khudaibergenov, "Uluchshat' deyatel'nost' apparata upravleniya," *Sovety deputatov trudyashchikhsya* (May 1977). The classic western study of this phenomenon is Jerry Hough's *The Soviet Prefects* (Cambridge, Mass.: Harvard University Press, 1969).

15. Popkov, *Etika,* pp. 187-198.

16. *Ibid.,* pp. 165-187. Roy Medvedev has offered an explanation for the personality cult of Stalin in terms of Stalin, the consumate bureaucrat, projecting an image of father-protector who defends the powerless citizen against the abuses of the bureaucratic machine. The system which built and sustains bureaucracy is then manifest to consciousness as an anti-bureaucratic savior. (Medvedev calls this "feeding on its own excrement.") It would appear that the Party collectively has sought to maintain this image. See Medvedev's *Kniga o sotsialisticheskoi demokratii* (Amsterdam and Paris: Alexander Herzen Foundation, 1972), esp. p. 53.

17. Since this is inconceivable in a "socialist" society, the ill-effects of bureaucracy are generally attributed to "survivals of bourgeois mentality." See, for instance, G. E. Glezerman, *Stroitel'stve kommunizma i razvitie obshchestvennykh otnoshenii* (Moscow: Nauka, 1966), p. 34.

18. Leonid Volkov, "Standards of Political Behavior and Perfection of the Management and Administration of Developed Socialist Society." (Paper presented at the Eleventh World Congress of the International Political Science Association, Moscow, August 12-18, 1979).

19. *Ibid.,* pp. 13-14.

20. Yu. A. Tikhomirov, "Vazhneishii dokument epokhi," *Sovety deputatov trudyashichikhsya* (August 1977).

21. B. Lazarev, "Vlast' i upravlenie," *Sovety narodnykh deputatov* (February 1978).

22. *Ibid.,* pp. 20-21.

23. Quoted in Carol W. Lewis and Stephen Sternheimer, *Soviet Urban Management* (New York: Praeger, 1979), p. 11.

24. *Kardy apparata upravleniya v SSSR* (Leningrad: Nauka, 1970), pp. 49-50.

25. Popkov, *Etika,* p. 94.

26. See their "Pravovoi status sluzhashchego" in *Sluzhashchii sovetskogo gosudarstvennogo apparata,* ed., Yu. A. Tikhomirov (Moscow: Yuridicheskaya literatura, 1970), p. 49.

27. O. V. Kozlova, *Tekhnika, tekhnologiya i kadry upravleniya proizvodstvom* (Moscow: Ekonomika, 1973), p. 68.

28. Afanas'ev in Afanas'ev, *Nauchnoe upravlenie*, p. 12.
29. Lebin and Perfil'ev, *Kadry*, pp. 33, 34.
30. F. B. Sadykov, "O vzaimootnosheniyakh rukovoditelei i mass" in Afanas'ev, *Nauchnoe upravlenie obshchestvom*, p. 62.
31. D. Gvishiani, *Organization and Management* (Moscow: Progress Publishers, 1972), p. 85.
32. Tikhomirov, "Vazhneishii dokument," pp. 16, 17; see, also Lebin and Perfil'ev, *Kadry*, pp. 65, 121; Popkov, *Etika*, pp. 35-38.
33. Yu. A. Rozenbaum, "Etiko-psikhologicheskie voprosy v rabote gosudarstvennykh sluzhashchikh," Tikhomirov, *Sluzhashchii*, pp. 30, 31.
34. Sadykov, "O vzaimootnosheni," p. 60; Lebin and Perfil'ev, *Kadry*, pp. 30, 31.
35. Popkov, *Etika*.
36. I. L. Bachilo, "Organizatsiya truda sluzhashchikh" in Tikhomirov, *Sluzhashchii*, p. 139.
37. E.g., Popkov, *Etika*, pp. 34, 97, 110-111.
38. I. Borisova, "Dushevnaya shedrost' ", *Izvestia* (June 11, 1978), p. 2.
39. Ibid.
40. Lebin and Perfil'ev, *Kadry*, p. 117.
41. N. I. Lapin, *Rukovoditel' kollektiva* (Moscow: Politizdat, 1974), pp. 22, 23.
42. Borisova, "Dushevnaya shedrost' ".
43. V. M. Manokhin, *Sovetskaya gosudarstvennaya sluzhba* (Moscow: Yuridicheskaya literatura, 1966), p. 126.
44. *Kadry*, p. 155.
45. Bachilo, "Organizatsiya truda," p. 97.
46. Lebin and Perfil'ev, *Kadry*, p. 117.
47. Popkov, *Etika*, p. 4.
48. Karpushin, *Nauchnyi kommunizm*, p. 265.
49. See his "intelligentsiya i sluzhashchie v usloviyakh stoitel'stva kommunizma," Glezerman, *stroitel'stvo kommunizma*, p. 162.
50. R. A. Safarov, "Mestnye sovety i organy obshchestvennoi samodeyatel'nosti," *Mestnye sovety na sovremennom etape*, ed., D. A. Gaidukov and N. G. Starovoitov (Moscow: Nauka, 1965), p. 306.
51. Popkov, *Etika*, pp. 40-47.
52. See his "Traditional, Market and Organizational Societies and the USSR," *World Politics*, vol. 16 (July 1964).
53. Rozenbaum, "Etiko-psikhologicheskie," p. 204.
54. Popkov, *Etika*, p. 16.
55. *Soviet Marxism* (New York: Vintage Books, 1961), pp. 79-80.
56. Quoted in Tony Cliff's *State Capitalism in Russia* (London: Pluto Press, 1974), pp. 122, 123.
57. In *The Essential Stalin*, ed., B. Franklin (London: Croom Helm, 1973), p. 387.
58. Marcuse, *Soviet Marxism*, pp. 109-116.
59. Lebin and Perfil'ev, *Kadry*, pp. 22-29; esp., p. 29.
60. Manokhin, *Sovetskaya*, pp. 16, 17; see also, pp. 92, 93.

61. Afanas'ev in Afanas'ev, *Nauchnoe upravlenie*, p. 5, 6.

62. On the problem which Krushchev's innovation sought to solve, and the problems which it created, see Roger E. Kanet, "The Rise and Fall of the All People's State," *Soviet Studies*, vol. 20 (July 1968). See also George A. Brinkley's, "Krushchev Remembered: On the Theory of Soviet Statehood," *Soviet Studies*, vol. 24 (January 1973).

63. M. A. Suslov, *Na putyakh stroitel'stva kommunizma* (vol. 2; Moscow: Politzdat, 1977), pp. 285-286.

64. K. F. Sheremet, "Novyi etap razvitiya demokratii sotsializma," *Izvestia* (March 4, 1978).

65. K. F. Sheremet, "Torzhestvo Leninskikh idei narodovlastiya," *Sovety deputatov trudyashchikhsya* (May 1977).

66. Afanas'ev, *Nauchnyi kommunizm*, pp. 194-196.

67. Manokhin, *Sovetskaya*, p. 14.

68. Popkov, *Etika*, pp. 4, 100.

69. Afanas'ev, *Nauchnyi*, p. 325.

70. Volkov, "Standards," uses precisely this word (p. 10).

71. For examples of this view, see B. N. Topornin, *Aktual'nye teoreticheskie problemy razvitiya gosudarstvennogo prava i sovetskogo stroitel'stva* (Moscow: Institut gos. i prava, AN, SSSR, 1976), pp. 5-17; esp., p. 11; E. Murav'ev, "Uchityvaya mnenie mass," *Izvestia* (March 3, 1979).

On the topic of the role of public opinion in the affairs of state generally, see R. A. Safarov, *Obshchestvennoe mnenie i gosudarstvennoe upravlenie* (Moscow: Yuridicheskaya literatura, 1975).

72. Afanas'ev, *Nauchnyi kommunizm*, pp. 327-8.

73. Popkov, *Etika*, p. 75.

74. Ibid.; Afanas'ev, *Nauchnyi kommunizm*, pp. 231, 268.

75. Karpushin, *Nauchnyi kommunizm*, pp. 249-255.

76. Afanas'ev, *Nauchnyi kommunizm*, pp. 257-258, 303-6.

77. Ibid., p. 277.

78. *Izvestia* (Jan. 25, 1977).

79. Manokhin, *Sov. gos. sluzhba*, p. 14; A. Lashin, "Massy upravlyayut," *Sovety deputatov trudyashchikhsya*, No. 9 (September 1969), pp. 7-12.

80. Rachkov, *Rol' nauki*, p. 135.

81. Yu. A. Kozlov, *Sootnoshenie gosudarstvennogo i obshchestvennogo upravleniya sotsialisticheskoi ekonomikoi* (Moscow: Misl', 1973), p. 136; *Izvestia* (May 28, 1977), p. 2.

82. Karpushin, *Nauchnyi kommunizm*, p. 216; A. M. Omarov, *Nauchnye osnovy upravleniya sotsialisticheskoi ekonomikoi* (Moscow: Misl', 1973), p. 136; *Izvestia* (May 28, 1977), p. 2.

83. Afanas'ev (*Nauchnyi kommunizma*, pp. 252-257) has given some thought to the spectre haunting industrial society which has been forecast by many writers of science fiction; viz., the problem of machines taking over. However, he has chosen to interpret their hyperbolic metaphor in a literal sense, i.e., as the machines physically replacing mankind. He is certainly, therefore, on solid ground when he answers in the negative.

84. Lazarev and Luk'yanov, "Vlast demokratiya," p. 15
This same view is expressed by L. I. Umanskii, "V. I. Lenin ob organizatorskoi deyatel'nosti i organizatorskikh sposobnostykh," *Voprosy psikhologii*, No. 2 (March/April 1963); V. M. Chikhikvadze, *The State, Democracy and
Legality in the USSR* (Moscow: Progress Publishers, 1973), pp. 127-128.

Conclusions and Implications

1. Juergen Habermas, *Legitimation Crisis* (Boston: Beacon, 1975); and,
idem, *Communication and the Evolution of Society* (Boston: Beacon, 1979).
2. Christopher Lasch, "Democracy and the 'Crisis of Confidence' ",
Democracy, vol. 1 (January 1981).
3. Colin Sumner, *Reading Ideologies* (London: Academic Press, 1979), p.
237.
4. Alvin W. Gouldner, *The Dialectic of Ideology and Technology* (New York:
Seabury, 1976) pp. 155-158.

INDEX

Academics, 81, 86, 125, 127, 129; in USA, 84-85, 100-03; in USSR 81-83, 118, 120-23
Academy of the National Economy, 62
Action research, 74
Administration, 25, 30, 38, 53, 86, 128; as democratic, 95, 108, 122; external contradiction of, 87, 89, 90, 126-27; general ideology of, 26, 126; internal contradiction of, 46, 54, 86, 126; language of, 25; orthodox theorists of, 39-40, 54, 71; practice of, 46, 126; professional literature on, xi, 35, 79, 81, 99, 106-09, 127; as representative, 95-100, 108-10; as scientific, 38, 59, 61, 64, 65, 108-09; special ideologies of, 35, 39-42, 126. *See also* Bureaucracy; Management
Administrative ideology, xi, 10, 13, 15-16, 21, 26-31, 35, 39, 50, 63, 70, 86-91, 98; humane form of, 49, 71-75, 86; of leadership, 47, 54, 64; Soviet version of, 29, 37, 53, 62, 109, 113-14. *See also* Administrative leadership; Ideology
Administrative leadership, 61-63, 72, 86, 90, 95; as creative, 63, 111, 127; as democratic, 90-95; as result of innate qualities, 64-65. See also *Rukovoditel'*
Administrators, xiii, 25, 29, 33-39, 45-47, 56, 61, 63, 69-71, 85, 89-92, 98-103; as apolitical 96; as generalists, 62; information for, 76, 83, 97; new type of, 75; in USSR, 62, 78. See also *Rukovoditel'*
Afanas'ev, V. G., 117
Alienation, 39-40, 126
American Academy for Public Administration, 92
Aron, Raymond, 18-19, 22
Artificial intelligence, 55
Authority: administrative interest in, 45-47; as formal, 61, 67, 73, 86, 127; as personal, 65, 86, 127
Automation, 56-57, 117-18

Bachilo, I. L., 112
Bannock, Graham, 58
Barnard, Chester A., 63
Barnum, D. T., 94
Bendix, Reinhard, 41, 45, 56
Bolsheviks, 30, 31
Bolshevik Revolution. *See* October Revolution
Braverman, Harry, 19
Bright, J. R., 57
Brown, Hedy, 67
Bureau of National Affairs, 69
Bureaucracy, 18-20, 23, 26-27, 40-41, 89, 125; as democratic, 95-100; external contradiction of, 89-90, 105, 118; internal contradiction of, 46, 54, 59, 61, 75-76, 79, 89. *See also* Administration
Bureaucratic collectivism, 29
Bureaucratic ideology, 3-5, 15, 23-24, 58, 61. *See also* Administrative ideology
Bureaucratization, 4, 23
Burnham, John, 28

Capitalism, 17, 23, 26, 53; state monopoly form of, 28; ideology of, 84, 127-29
Capitalist economy. *See* Capitalism
Capitalist society. *See* Capitalism
Carlo, Antonio, 29
Carpentier, J., 67
Cassirer, Ernst, 7
Chandler, Alfred D., Jr., 30
Change agents, 57, 74, 96, 99-100
Citizens, 32, 33, 129; in USA, 90-91, 100-02; in USSR, 109, 116, 122
City council, 93, 95, 97, 101-02
City manager, 93, 95, 97, 101-02
Class domination, 109-10
Class relations, 17. *See also* class struggle
Class structure, 22, 29
Class struggle, 17, 20-21, 46, 125
Cocks, Paul, 55
Commission Plan, 93
Communications theory, 56
Communism, 26, 52-53, 57, 105, 113-14,